For ... ll

In grateful ...ks

[signature]

November 1967.

Lind Cally
London
12/77

HASSAN

The Story of Hassan of Bagdad and how he came to make the Golden Journey to Samarkand

THE DRAMA LIBRARY
General Editor: Edward Thompson

HASSAN

by

JAMES ELROY FLECKER

An acting edition prepared
and introduced by
BASIL DEAN

HEINEMANN

LONDON

Heinemann Educational Books Ltd
LONDON MELBOURNE TORONTO
SINGAPORE CAPE TOWN
AUCKLAND IBADAN
HONG KONG

FIRST PUBLISHED 1922

REPRINTED 1922 (twice), 1923 (four times), 1924
(three times), 1926, 1928, 1930, 1931, 1932,
1933, 1935, 1936, 1937, 1939, 1941,
1946 (twice), 1947

REVISED EDITION, FIRST PUBLISHED IN
THE DRAMA LIBRARY 1951
REPRINTED 1960, 1962, 1966

*This play, arranged for the stage and produced by Basil Dean,
with music by Frederick Delius, scene and costume designs by
George W. Harris and Ballets by Michael Fokine, was presented on Thursday, September 20th, 1923, at His Majesty's
Theatre, London, by George Grossmith and J. A. E. Malone,
by arrangement with ReandeaN.*

PUBLISHED BY
HEINEMANN EDUCATIONAL BOOKS LTD
48 CHARLES STREET, LONDON W.I
PRINTED IN GREAT BRITAIN BY
BOOKPRINT LIMITED, CRAWLEY, SUSSEX

CONTENTS

CHARACTERS

HASSAN, a Confectioner

THE CALIPH HAROUN AL RASCHID

ISHAK, his Minstrel

JAFAR, his Vizier

MASRUR, his Executioner

RAFI, King of the Beggars

SELIM, a Friend of Hassan's

THE CAPTAIN OF THE MILITARY

THE CHIEF OF THE POLICE

ALI
ABDU } Nondescripts

ALDER
WILLOW
JUNIPER
TAMARISK } Slave Boys

THE PORTER of Yasmin's House

THE CHINESE PHILOSOPHER

A DERVISH

THE FOUNTAIN GHOST

A HERALD

THE PRISON GUARDS

PERVANEH

YASMIN

Various AMBASSADORS, a WRESTLER, a CALIGRAPHIST, a JESTER, GHOSTS, MUTES, DANCING WOMEN, BEGGARS, SOLDIERS, POLICE, ATTENDANTS and CASUAL LOITERERS.

Programme of the First Performance of the Play in English*
at His Majesty's Theatre, London, on September 20th, 1923.

George Grossmith and J. A. E. Malone's Production of

HASSAN

The Story of Hassan and how he came to make the Golden
Journey to Samarkand

A Play in Five Acts by

JAMES ELROY FLECKER

Arranged for Production on the Stage by Basil Dean

The Characters in the Order of their Appearance:

HASSAN, a Confectioner	Mr. Henry Ainley
SELIM	Mr. S. Esme Percy
YASMIN	Miss Cathleen Nesbitt
A PORTER	Mr. Sydney Bland
THE CALIPH, Haroun Al Raschid	Mr. Malcolm Keen
ISHAK, his Ministrel	Mr. Leon Quartermaine
JAFAR, his Vizier	Mr. Frank Cochrane
MASRUR, his Executioner	Mr. Edmund Willard
RAFI, King of the Beggars	Mr. Basil Gill
ALDER	Miss Rita Page
WILLOW } Slaves	Miss Kitty McCoy
JUNIPER	Miss Maureen Dillon
TAMARISK	Miss Eileen Raven
TWO BEGGAR {	Mr. Nicholas Nadegin
LEADERS {	Mr. Robert East
ALI } Nondescripts	Mr. Ivor Barnard
ABDU	Mr. Andrew Leigh
THE CHIEF OF THE POLICE	Mr. Alfred Clark
THE CAPTAIN OF THE MILITARY	Mr. Tarver Penna
A HERALD	Mr. Douglas Burbidge
PERVANEH	Miss Laura Cowie

* The World Première took place in a German translation at Darmstad
in June, 1923, in which Mr. Frederick Valk created the part of Hassan.

Characters at the Caliph's Court:

THE PRINCE OF BASRA	Mr. Frank Vosper
THE PRINCE OF DAMASCUS	Mr. Claude Delaval
THE PRINCE OF KONIAH	Mr. Osborn Adair
THE GOVERNOR OF KHORASAN	Mr. Harrison Lawson
A CALIGRAPHIST	Mr. Thomas Waters
A WRESTLER	Mr. B. E. Evremonde
ABU NOWAS, the Caliph's Jester	Mr. Sidney Bland
THE RAJAH OF THE UPPER GANGES	Mr. C. R. Stone
THE CHINESE PHILOSOPHER	Mr. Ivor Barnard
A DERVISH	Mr. Caton-Woodville
THE AMBASSADOR OF THE EMPRESS IRENE	Mr. Vivian Carew

Characters in the Last Poem:

HASSAN	Mr. Henry Ainley
ISHAK	Mr. Leon Quartermaine
THE MASTER OF THE CARAVAN	Mr. S. Esme Percy
THE CHIEF DRAPER	Mr. Frank Vosper
THE CHIEF GROCER	Mr. Douglas Burbidge
THE PRINCIPAL JEW	Mr. Tarver Penna
THE WATCHMAN	Mr. Frank Cochrane
A WOMAN	Miss Dartrey
AN OLD MAN	Mr. Charles R. Stone

Soldiers, Police, Dancing Women, Beggars, Mutes, Attendants, Merchants, Camel Drivers, Jews, Pilgrims, Torturers, Casual Loiterers:

Messrs. Talbot Homewood, R. D. Whitaker, Eric Fowler, James Lomas, G. Dunstall, Laurence Attridge, Roy Leaker, Roy Rich, G. Bailey, Mesdames Evelyn Taylor, Fabia Drake.

Members of the Ballet:

Messrs. George Wolkowsky, Jack Triesalt, Jack Renshaw, L. Lucas, W. Scott, Aubrey Hitchins, Leon Kelloway, Alex. Artirov, Keith Lester, Caird Leslie. Mesdames Ann Tewksbury, Peggy Mackenzie, Ursula Moreton, B. Ostrehan, Dyta Morena, Audrey Carlyon, Rosalind Wade, Vera Temple, Margot St. Ledger, Renee Gadd, Vivienne Bennett, Helene Saxova, Joane Wolfe, Eliane Ferrars, Babette Moore.

The Music composed by Frederick Delius

The Scenery and Costumes designed by
George W. Harris

The Ballets arranged by Michel Fokine

The whole Production planned and rehearsed by
BASIL DEAN

THE SCENES

ACT I

ACT II

ACT III

INTRODUCTION

By Basil Dean

I

HASSAN first came to my notice in rather casual fashion.
One morning in the autumn of 1913 there was deposited on
my office desk in His Majesty's Theatre a bulky package that
had all the outward appearance of being just one more of
those voluminous outpourings that it was part of my lot to
read. Reporting on plays which the management already
considered hopeless was one of the whimsical duties that
Sir Herbert Tree assigned to me when I joined his staff,
ostensibly as an 'assistant producer', but in practice as a
'snatcher-up' of any inconsiderable task likely to keep at bay
my youthful sense of frustration. The package was accompanied by a characteristic and hastily scribbled note from
Viola Tree, saying, 'please give this wonderful play special
attention; I can't get Daddy to read it as he says it's too
long.' 'The Chief', the friendly but properly subservient
title by which Tree was known to his staff, disliked reading
plays in manuscripts. He preferred to have them read to
him, if they were being seriously considered for production
that is, usually with a number of executives present and to
the accompaniment of witty but disconcerting comments
and a ceaselessly active pencil and paper, with which he
passed round the table his vague suggestions for dresses and
scenery. I believe he did read *Hassan* eventually, following
an enthusiastic report; but he continued to grumble at its
length and finally decided that the part would not suit him.

Matters could not be allowed to rest there. Even in draft form, the play was clearly of major importance. With the help of Edward Marsh, enthusiastic supporter of the group of young Georgian poets then giving expression to the artistic impulses of the new century, I extracted a promise from the Chief to reconsider the play when it had been brought into shape. I then got into touch with Flecker and reached an understanding to give him what help I could in reducing the manuscript to manageable proportions and in steering it through subsequent production. His early death converted this confident promise on my part into a moral obligation, one which I have done my best to discharge through the years. But at the time I knew nothing of the desperate efforts the poet was making to hold on to life until he should see his masterpiece fulfilled before an audience.

Encouraged by the prospect of eventual production and possibly with a sub-conscious sense that time was all too short for him, Flecker began the work of revision at once without waiting for my technical recommendations. These I sent on to him at Davos where he had now gone to live. Then I began the task of cutting my copy of the play, a process to which I gave much care and thought, for the feeling was strong within me that injudicious work might damage a masterpiece. Thus, the work was proceeding on two fronts simultaneously, as it were. Eventually, these two revised versions crossed each other in the post, but that was not until some months later.

As the work progressed, Flecker and I were both anxious for personal contact; he in order to speed up the work, and I to meet a young poet of my own generation whose work I so deeply admired. In the spring of 1914 I wrote and told him I was shortly getting married. As he and his wife were staying at Locarno for a few weeks in the same month, we planned our honeymoon trip to take us there first, the Fleckers agreeing to wait for us. Shortly before leaving England I received an urgent letter from him asking me to hasten my arrival as he was afraid he could not stay in the Italian Lakes much longer. With the advance of spring the climate became warm and relaxing; this was making him ill again. When my wife and I eventually reached Locarno he had gone back into the mountains, leaving a pathetic little note begging me to visit him in Davos for a few days. I felt this to be impossible under the circumstances, and, evading my wife's inquiries as to my sudden preoccupation, secretly wrote off my regrets. I felt this was a decision a bride should not be asked to share. Had I recognised it as my last opportunity of seeing him alive I might have acted differently. However, that is the commonest of clichés; to say that if we could see into the future our actions would be different. . . . Thus it was that from first to last my contact with Flecker was by correspondence alone.

Meanwhile, Flecker's friends in London made careful plans so that when the work of revision was completed Tree's interest should be caught and held. This was to be done by telling him of the immense interest which the new *Hassan* had aroused in a rival managerial breast. It seemed the best way to appeal to his somewhat acquisitive nature. Alas! this amiable conspiracy was knocked on the head by the outbreak of the First World War. And when peace came again both manager and poet were dead. . . .

II

SOME LETTERS

Very few of Flecker's letters to me survived the domestic upheavals and removals of two world wars; but here is one that he wrote at the time of forwarding the first corrected manuscript:

Hotel Buol, Davos Platz, Switzerland.

18th June, 1914.

DEAR MR. DEAN,

I am sending you by the same mail my revised *Hassan*! I cannot help thinking that it is so immensely improved that it will require very little alteration; but of course I will be very amenable. Only you must not blame me for wanting to improve my work as far as possible myself before sending it to you.

Please never think that I want to institute a sort of Literature *v*. Drama quarrel! For me every correction that makes the play more actable makes it better literature. The play I send you now is the play I shall publish.

Please write in red ink or pencil (on opposite side) on my MS all your observations and/or the corrections or cuts you still wish me to make and return me the MS when ready.

I am very glad indeed that you are so much nearer certainty about the play. I should like to know however whether you have given up the idea of shewing it to Tree.* I have a vague idea that if Tree produces a play with the vaguest shadow of merit its an immense financial success—because people come to see him in any case.

* Flecker was told that Tree had agreed to read the revised manuscript.

I must thank you at all events for pushing along *Hassan* so splendidly.

Can we have *real camels* for the final scene?

I shall come to London to see a performance if I have to come on a stretcher. I hope to be able to have a marvellous operation soon which effects a real cure. It's pretty damnable being so hopelessly ill just when at last there's a prospect of some real success.

Yours very sincerely,
JAMES ELROY FLECKER.

Here is another letter which, although it is undated, must have reached me just before Flecker tackled the final revision

Hotel Buol, Davos Platz, Switzerland.
Friday.

DEAR MR. DEAN,

Would you be so very kind as to let me have your corrected copy of *Hassan* as soon as possible. I upset myself badly hurrying over the last revision and I want to have as much leisure as possible to correct the work finally. I shall be very careful to carry out your suggestions. I should, I must say, very much like an appreciation of my revision, as I worked at it very hard.

I should also be very interested to hear a little more about the arrangements you have made or hope to make with regard to producing the play yourself.

You will very likely want to preserve some passages I have omitted.

Do let me have a line if you have as yet any leisure.

Yours very sincerely,
JAMES ELROY FLECKER.

A letter which reached me at an Army training camp after the war broke out shows that Flecker's thoughts were still concentrated upon improving the play. He had sent me his second revision, but longed for some message of hope about the possibility of production to encourage him to improve the work still more. I could not give it to him.

> Maison Baratelli, Davos Platz, Switzerland.
> 12th October.

DEAR MR. DEAN,

Should like a line from you just to know how the theatrical world is. I suppose you intend not to think again of *Hassan* till after the War.

(Post is quite safe—7 days.) You can very well return me *Hassan* in a registered packet if you like. I should like to have it with me and finish it off. Alas, if I could only get well enough in a year's time to see it played I wouldn't mind the delay. However we have a flat of our own now which makes life easier.

> Yours very sincerely,
> JAMES ELROY FLECKER.

The last communication I received was dated 29th November, by which time I was deep in camp mud, probing the mysteries of *The Manual of Infantry Training*. It consisted of a postcard written and overwritten, partly in ink and partly in pencil. Evidently I had expressed doubt about the wisdom of sending the manuscript through the post in wartime.

Maison Baratelli, Davos Platz, Switzerland.
29th November.

MY DEAR DEAN,

Send it by ordinary or even unregistered *MS post*. Didn't I tell you the post was absolutely safe. I haven't lost a parcel, sample, letter or newspaper since the outbreak of war and that with a biggish correspondence.

Only do get my permanent address right. I've got a pleasant flat where I shall probably lie up for many a day to come. Best luck.

Ever yours,
J. E. FLECKER.

I take responsibility of post. I've got another copy of my corrected *Hassan*. That's at Munich—but quite safe. War will soon be over. You'll get about March photos of scenes from *Hassan* on model stage.

Hassan, a tragedy, *might* be the thing for a not *too* pressed country in war time. But the war'll be over in 6 months—mark me!

Ever yours,
J. E. F.

My responsibility *re* postage.
(Pen note at top of card):
No letter inside: shut but don't seal: register.
Mark it *Papiers d'Affaires*—2½d. the lb. it costs.

(Pencil notes on card):
Everything comes here regular in 8 days including parcel post.
Cheques changed 25–15 the pound. Trains here and through France safe.

Why don't you come out and winter sport. Prices of all
food regular. Trains only 36 hrs. from Paris. All the
poor devils who *need* Davos holding back thro' funk:
pitiable: have written papers.

What ass wouldn't insure *Hassan*? If the P.O. it wasn't for
War reasons.
Ignorance in England of Continental conditions absurd.

————

This disjointed communication shows all too clearly the
anxiety and strain from which Flecker was suffering. The
manuscript must have been returned to him because
although he continued to work on it until within a week or
so of his death, which occurred on January 3rd, 1915, at the
age of thirty-one, he failed to complete his self-imposed
task. The final version that I received after the War con-
tained numerous corrections in the first half of the play,
some in Flecker's handwriting and some in that of his wife;
but there were none at all in the later scenes. . . . The play
was first published in 1922, using Flecker's first revision.
When it reached the stage one year later the acting version
included all the author's last-minute cuts and alterations.
And it is that version which is here published for the first
time.

III

The promises made so light-heartedly before the War
came heavily home to roost after the Armistice. All through
the exciting first years of the ReandeaN Company, when

success and failure chased each other in violent contrast across our chosen path, my unfulfilled promise to Flecker was never far from my mind. The sense of moral obligation was increased by my having asked Flecker's literary executor to postpone printing the play until its production on the stage had been arranged, so as not to prejudice its chances with the managers. Plays that are published beforehand remain stillborn nine times out of ten.

A first-class London production was an expensive matter. It was outside the scope and policy of the ReandeaN organisation. His Majesty's Theatre was the most suitable home for it; but the firm of Grossmith and Malone, who now owned the lease of the theatre, seemed to be interested mainly in the production of musical comedies. Then one day they announced their intention of restoring Tree's old home to its former pre-eminence. This proved to be a stroke of good fortune, one of those unexpected happenings that make life in the theatre so fascinating to all who obey its call. The new management invited me to produce Somerset Maugham's *East of Suez* for them. This was a great success. During the run I had an operation for appendicitis. One day both Grossmith and Malone came to see me at the hospital. I can still see them standing, one at either side of my bed, whilst Grossmith with much charm and circumlocution broached the purpose of their visit. Encouraged by success, he had visions of making His Majesty's the first theatre in the land. Who knows? Possibly he might receive official recognition if he also made himself its active (and acting) head. And so to the point: Would I direct a revival of Arthur Pinero's *The Gay Lord Quex* with himself as the gay lord? Instantly it flashed through my mind that here was the opportunity at last. I said: 'Yes, I will do it for you if you promise to do *Hassan* immediately afterwards.' The unusual bargain was struck there and then, although I had great difficulty later on in persuading Grossmith that his appearance in the name part was not a part of it.

As the day of production drew near public anticipation rose like a fever. Indeed, old playgoers remarked that nothing comparable had occurred since the great days of Irving and Tree. And the only recent equivalent would be, I suppose, the public excitement over the work of the Old Vic when Olivier and Richardson headed the Company, and, more recently still, the international reputation achieved by the Shakespeare Memorial Theatre at Stratford-upon-Avon.

James Barrie was with me throughout the long dress rehearsal smoking his biggest pipe and saying never a word. When he returned to his flat in Adelphi Terrace long after midnight, he sat down to write me a eulogistic prophecy of the approaching night's events, one which I look back upon with some wistfulness, for, as near as I can remember it, he ended his letter by saying: 'To-night you will have such a night in the theatre as never again in your life.' So, the play came to the stage of His Majesty's Theatre after all; to be precise, on 20th September, 1923, before one of the most distinguished audiences that had ever assembled there, including most of the leading dramatists of the day. It was eight years after the poet's death.

Plays about the East, especially one with the poetic quality of *Hassan*, can be effectively presented in various ways and with varying degrees of sumptuousness. Scanning the Press criticisms of that first production, one perceives here and there some expressions of regret that the play had not been more simply done. Now Flecker was not a modernist; he was a romantic. This is clearly shown not only in his choice of subject but in all the sensuous delights of eye and ear to which he gives such passionate expression in the play. And he would have rejoiced in the mellifluous sounds provided by Delius in a musical score that will remain as closely identified with the work as is the music of Grieg with *Peer Gynt*. The surroundings of his daily life, the filthy streets, slaughtered animals black with flies hanging amidst the dust of the bazaars, the Ford cars and bowler hats, the passport offices and scurrilous newspapers, all the sordidness of existence in the modern Consular Service irked him greatly. Indeed, at one time he longed to get away from it all and to return home. But he had a nostalgia and a panache for the colour, the lust and the cruelty of the East as it existed in the illustrated pages of *One Thousand and One Nights*. This in mind, I felt justified in my attempt to recreate the luxurious, not to say gaudy quality of the East of popular legend. Embellishment could neither hide nor smother the lyrical beauty of the writing; rather did it help the general atmosphere of sensuous dreaming in which the work was originally conceived.

Nevertheless, it would be impossible to reproduce satisfactorily the conception of a quarter of a century ago, even if one wished to do so. Changes within oneself would prevent that, quite apart from the changes in public taste. And so when I produced the play recently for the National Theatre Organisation of South Africa I did it quite simply on a partly curtained stage: yet the magic of Flecker's words remained. Now in the Festival of Britain 1951 production a style reminiscent of the old Persian and Indo-Persian miniatures has been chosen; by these means the essential Arabian Nights atmosphere of the Flecker story can be preserved without clouding his limpid prose or smothering his verse. In future it should be possible for Repertory Theatres, Drama Groups and other acting companies to achieve satisfactory results by the simplest means, and to give their audiences an opportunity of hearing Flecker's glittering lines spoken upon the stage instead of reading them in the study, a compromise with which his admirers have had to rest content for too long.

A fresh examination of the various manuscripts in my possession shows unmistakably how Flecker was teaching himself the craft of writing for the theatre as he went along. The process of compression only ceased just before his death, when the ebbing of his strength took away all power of further work. In this acting version it will be noted that the scene in the House of the Moving Walls (Act I, Scene III), and the encounter between Hassan and Yasmin in the Pavilion (Act II, Scene I), both show last minute revisions; and there are minor improvements in several of the Caliph's later speeches. But if the poet had had more time the two separate stories that go to make up the play, i.e., the farce of the lovesick confectioner and his Yasmin, and the tragedy of the two young lovers condemned to a cruel choice by a vicious Caliph, would no doubt have been more closely welded together to make up the tragic farce that became the final expression of his romanticism. If his revisions had extended to those closing scenes of the play wherein Ishak returns to find Hassan lying beneath the fountain in the Caliph's Garden, half-crazed with horror at the suffering he has been forced to witness, and to the ensuing scene between the Ghosts, it is probable that the gap remaining between the interwoven stories would have been closed completely, possibly by relating more closely Ishak's decision to undertake the pilgrimage to the suffering of Hassan. As it is the play may leave the impression of 'a broken back' with the casual reader, but the defect is not apparent in performance when the full emotional impact of the Ghost Scene is realised. Here the author was right in believing that this most moving scene would provide a bridge for the emotions of the audience to pass from the scalding terror of the Torture Scene to the bracing upper air of the joyous Last Pilgrimage.

When all is said there is no doubt that by his premature death, England lost a great dramatic poet in Flecker. In his short life of thirty-one years he had had time to do no more than spread the wings of his poetic fancy. Yet he left behind him a play of lasting memory.

THE STORY OF HASSAN OF BAGDAD

ACT I

SCENE 1

SCENE: *A room 'behind the shop' in old Bagdad. In the background a large caldron steaming, for the shop is a sweet-stuff shop and the sugar is boiling. The room has little furniture beyond a carpet, old but unexpectedly choice, and some Persian hangings (geometrical designs, with crude animals and some verses from the Koran hand-painted on linen). A ramshackle wooden partition in one corner shuts off from the living-room what appears to be the shop.*

Squatting on the carpet—facing each other:

Hassan, the Confectioner, 45, rotund, moustache, turban, greasy grey dress.

Selim, his friend, young, vulgarly handsome, gaudily clothed.

HASSAN (*rocking on his mat*):   Eywallah, Eywallah!

SELIM: Thirty-seven times have you made the same remark, O father of repetition.

HASSAN (*more dolefully than ever*):   Eywallah, Eywallah!

SELIM: Have you caught fever? Is your chest narrow, or your belly thunderous?

HASSAN (*with a ponderous sigh*):   Eywallah!

SELIM: Is that the merchant of sweetmeats, that sour face? O poisoner of children, surely it would be better to cut the knot of reluctance and uncord the casket of explanation.

1

HASSAN (*inclining towards the mat*): None is good, save God. Know, Selim, that I am in love.

SELIM: In love! Then why sit moaning on the mat? Are there not beauties at the barbers, and lights of love at the bazaar?

HASSAN (*angrily*): Hold your tongue, Selim, or leave me. I was in earnest when I said I loved, and your coarseness is ill-fitting to my mood. And well I know I am Hassan, the Confectioner, yet I can love as sincerely as Mejnun; for assuredly she on whom my heart is bent is not less fair than Leila.

SELIM (*ironically*): Alas! I mistook the particular for the general, and did not recognise the purity of your intentions. But I would not mention Mejnun. Mejnun was young, and you are old, and he was a prince, and you are a confectioner, and he was beautiful, and you are not, and he was very thin because of his sorrow, and you are fatter than those four-legged I mention not—God curse their herdsmen!

HASSAN: And if it be as you say, Selim, if I am indeed a fat, old, ugly tradesman, have I not good reason to be sorry and rock upon my mat, for how shall I attain my heart's desire?

SELIM: Listen to me, Hassan, why is it that in this last year you have become different from the Hassan that was Hassan? From time to time you talk strangly in your cups, like a mad poet; and you have bought a lute and a carpet too fine for your house. And now I fear you are losing your senses when I hear this talk of love from one who is past the age of folly.

HASSAN: It may be so, young man. Indeed, I think I am a fool. It is the affliction of Allah.

2

SELIM: Tell me, at least, who she is.

HASSAN: Listen, Selim, and I will tell you my affair. Three
days ago a woman came here to buy loukoum of me,
dressed as a widow, and bade me follow her to her door
with the parcel. Alas, Selim! I could see her eyes
beneath the veil, and they were like the twin fountains
in the Caliph's garden; and her lips beneath her veil were
like roses hidden in moss, and her waist was flexible as a
palm-tree swaying in the wind, and her hips were large
and heavy and round, like water melons in the season of
water melons. And I glanced at her but she would not
smile, and I sighed but she would not glance, and the
door of her house shut fast against me, like the gate of
Paradise against an infidel. Eywallah!

        (*Recommences moaning.*)

SELIM: And where was the house of this widow who
bought sweetmeats and had none to sell?

HASSAN: In the street of Felicity, by the Fountain of the
Two Pigeons.

SELIM (*musing*):   It must be the widow of that Achmet they
hung last year by the Basra Gate.

HASSAN: Which Achmet?

SELIM: The hairy one. Well, take courage, faint heart,
since all things can be cured save perversity in asses.
Perhaps I can cure you of love.

HASSAN: By the Prophet, Selim, do not cure my love,
cure her indifference.

SELIM (*with sudden alertness*):   There is only one way of
doing that.

HASSAN: Which way?

SELIM: Do you believe in magic, Hassan?

HASSAN: Men who think themselves wise believe nothing

3

till the proof. Men who are wise believe anything till the disproof.

SELIM: What do we know if magic be a lie or not? But, since it is certain that only magic can avail you, you may as well put it to the test. You can buy a philtre that can draw her love, and send her a jar of magic sweets.

HASSAN: I am ready to do all things, ingenious Selim; but do you know a good magician?

SELIM: Zachariah, the Jew, has but lately arrived from Aleppo: he is the talk of all the market-place, and a wonderful man if tales be true.

HASSAN: Have you the tales?

SELIM: I have this among many. They say that in Bokhara a man called him an offensive Jew and flung a stone at his head: and he caused the stone to be suspended in the air and the man too, so that the man walked all round Bokhara over the heads of the passers-by, who, were astonished, and was constrained to enter his house by the upper window.

HASSAN (*incredulous*):   Mashallah!

SELIM: And stranger than that. At Ispahan men say he took off the dome of the Great Mosque and turned it round and had a bath in it, and put it back again.

HASSAN: Mashallah!

SELIM: And strangest of all, at Cairo, for the amusement of the Sultan, he turned the whole population into apes for half an hour.

HASSAN: A very trifling change if you knew the Egyptians. I don't believe a word of all these tales. Yet, doubtless he is good enough physician to make a love philtre. But are philtres any good?

SELIM: There can be no doubt that there are philtres

which drive women to love, though their hearts be as strong and their heads as cold as the mountains of Qaf. But as for this Zachariah, I know he sells philtres at ten dinars the bottle: his shop is crowded with rich old women.

HASSAN: Eywallah, Selim, I am sick of love; no damsel is worth ten dinars. And sages have remarked, 'The ideal is expensive!' and philosophers have observed, 'There are a thousand figs on the fig-tree and all as like as like.'

SELIM: What! All the smooth, shining hills and well-wooded valleys in that country of love . . . all going for ten dinars! . . . And this is the man whose love is like Mejnun's! What is ten dinars to a man in love? You gave thrice that sum for this carpet.

HASSAN: A carpet is a carpet, and a woman is a woman. It is not only the ten dinars. But you know that in this market I have a character. 'Hassan,' men say, 'is a safe man. Hassan will not leave his jacket on the wall, or buy peas without prodding the sack.' But if they hear: 'A stranger came to Bagdad and no Mussulman and said he would do this, and Hassan has paid him ten dinars and got no gain,' they will nudge each other when I walk abroad at evening, and say: 'A sad end'; and they will call out to me as they pass, 'Ya Hassan, give me ten dinars that I may build a mosque!' And I shall be shamed where I was honoured, and abased where I was exalted . . .

(*A loud knocking on the floor of the adjacent shop causes Hassan to retire thither hurriedly. As he disappears Yasmin peeps inquisitively, unveiled, through the little window in the partition.*)

SELIM: What an impudent little beauty. . . . Why, she

had a widow's scarf on. She must be the princess!
(*Rocks with laughter.*) The unattainable ideal! And I have
her address. It requires a frenzied lover to pay cash for
a flask of coloured water. But I doubt if Hassan's
sweets mingled with coloured water will do aught but
make her sick. Whereas a cake stuffed with those very
dinars. . . . Allah, the dinars would not choke her! O
thou fool Hassan!

> Tell not thy shirt who smiled and answered 'Yes':
> Dream not her name, nor fancy her address.

(*Enter Hassan, pale and staggering.*)

HASSAN: Selim, in the name of friendship, take these ten
dinars and buy me that philtre, and return with speed.

SELIM (*feigning irritation*):   Allah! Am I your messenger?
Go yourself to the Jew.

HASSAN: I must prepare the sweetmeats this very hour,
to send them to her before sunset. In the name of
friendship, Selim, take the dinars and purchase me the
philtre.

SELIM (*rising and taking dinars*):   Do not make me charge-
able, O Hassan, if the philtre is without effect. I only
repeat what I have heard.

HASSAN: No, I will not blame you. But go quickly for
the magic that nothing may be left unsampled that may
prove beneficial.

(*Exit Selim; Hassan makes up the fire and prepares his
caldron, saying meanwhile*)

That young man weareth out my carpet apace. I begin
to think also he doth fray the braid of my affection. But if
he buys me a good philtre I will forgive him. Oh, cruel
destiny, thou hast made me a common man with a common
trade. My friends are fellows from the market, and all my

worthless family is dead. Had I been rich, ah me! how deep had been my delight in matters of the soul, in poetry and music and pictures, and companions who do not jeer and grin, and above all, in the colours of rich carpets and expensive silks. But be content, O artist: thou hast one carpet; be content, O, confectioner: thou hast one love— one love, but unattained . . .

Now I will make her sweets, such sweets, ah me! as never I made in my life before. I will make her sweets like globes of crystal, like cubes of jade, like polygons of ruby. I will make her sweets like flowers. I will perfume my sweets with the perfume of roses, so that she shall say 'a rose'! and smell before she tastes. And in the heart of each flower I will distil one drop of the magic of love. Did I not say 'they shall be flowers'?

SCENE 2

SCENE: *Moonlight. The Street of Felicity by the Fountain of the Two Pigeons. A house with a balcony on either side of the street.*

In front of one of the houses, Hassan, cloaked: a Porter.

HASSAN: Has she received the box, O guardian of the door of separation?

PORTER: From my hands, O dispenser of bounty.

HASSAN: What did thy mistress say?

PORTER: Sir, the hands of mediation are empty.

HASSAN (*giving a dinar*):   I have filled them. What honey dropped from that golden mouth?

PORTER: She said—may thy servant find grace—'Curses on the fat sugar cook and his love-sick eyes. Allah be praised, his confectionery is better than his countenance!'

HASSAN (*aside*): If she likes the confectionery, all may be well. And did she eat the confectionery?

PORTER: I do not know. But within the hour I removed the box, and it was empty.

HASSAN: Ah! Salaam and thanks.

PORTER: And to thee the Salaam.

HASSAN: But tell me what is the name of thy mistress?

PORTER: Yasmin is her name, Sir.

HASSAN: A sweet name for a moonlight night. Salaam aleikum.

PORTER: Ya Hawaja, v'aleikum assalam!

(*The Porter returns and shuts the gate.*)

HASSAN (*to himself*): What if the Jews are an older race than we and know old forgotten secrets? Alas, I believe no more in these Israelitish sweets. And yet, who can say? The young men of the market-place laugh at all enchantments—but do they know how to spin the sun? On a night like this, does not the very fountain sing in tune and enchant the dropping stones? Ah, Yasmin? (*Taking out lute from beneath his cloak and tuning it.*) Yasmin . . . Yasmin . . . Yasmin . . . Yasmin.

(*Intones to the accompaniment of the lute.*)

How splendid in the morning glows the lily; with what grace he throws

His supplication to the rose: do roses nod the head, Yasmin?

But when the silver dove descends I find the little flower of friends,

Whose very name that sweetly ends, I say when I have
   said, Yasmin.

The morning light is clear and cold; I dare not in that
   light behold

A whiter light, a deeper gold, a glory too far shed,
   Yasmin.

But when the deep red eye of day is level with the lone
   highway,

And some to Meccah turn to pray, and I toward thy bed,
   Yasmin.

Or when the wind beneath the moon is drifting like a
   soul aswoon,

And harping planets talk love's tune with milky wings
   outspread, Yasmin,

Shower down thy love, O burning bright! for one night
   or the other night

Will come the Gardener in white, and gathered flowers
   are dead, Yasmin!

(*As Hassan intones the last 'Yasmin' with passion the shutters
   open, and Yasmin, veiled, looks out.*)

YASMIN: Alas, Minstrel, Yasmin is my name also, but it
was for a fairer Yasmin than me, I fear you have strung
these pearls.

HASSAN: There is no Yasmin but Yasmin, and you are
Yasmin.

YASMIN: Can this be Hassan, the Confectioner?

HASSAN: I am Hassan, and I am a confectioner.

YASMIN: Mashallah, Hassan, your words are sweeter than
your sweets.

HASSAN: Gracious lady, your eyes look down through
your veil like angels through a cloud. Dare I ask to see
your face, O bright perfection?

9

YASMIN (*roguishly*):   Do you take me for a Christian, father of impertinence? And since when do the daughters of Islam unveil before strangers?

HASSAN: It is said: he who speaks to the heart is no stranger.

YASMIN (*unveiling her eyes*):   Are you satisfied, O importunate!

HASSAN: Never, till I have seen perfection to perfection.

YASMIN: You would shrivel, my poet. What about 'the glory too far shed, Yasmin'?

HASSAN: Let me see you unveiled, Yasmin.

YASMIN: Anything to close the portal of your face. (*Unveiling.*) There. Do I please thee, my Sultan?

HASSAN (*rapturously*):   Oh, you are beautiful!

YASMIN: Prince of poets, is that all you have to say! Not even a hint that the heavens are opened, or that there are two moons in the sky together?

HASSAN: There is but one.

YASMIN: Well confectioned, my confectioner! And now, Good-night.

HASSAN: O stay, Yasmin, you are too beautiful and I too bold. I am nothing, and you are the Queen of the Stars of Night. But the thought of you is twisted in the strings of my heart; I burn with love of you, Yasmin. Put me to the proof, my lady; there is nothing I could not do for your bright eyes. I would cross the salt desert and wrest the cup of the water of life from the Jinn that guards it; I would walk to the barriers of the world and steal the roc's egg from its diamond nest. I would swim the seven oceans, and cross the five islands to rob Solomon ben Dawud of his ring in the palace where he lies sleeping in the silence and majesty of uncorrupting death. And I would slip the ring on your finger and make you mistress of the spirits of the air—but would you love me? Could you love me, do you love me, Yasmin?

YASMIN: There is love and love and love.

HASSAN (*passionately*): Oh, answer me!

YASMIN: I think I have been enchanted, Hassan; how, I cannot tell. Till this afternoon the thought of your appearance made my heart narrow with disgust. But since I ate your present of comfits—and they were admirable comfits, and I ate them with speed—my heart is changed and inclined toward you, I know not why or how, except it be through magic.

HASSAN (*aside*): She is mine, and magic rules the world! (*Aloud*): Yasmin, shall I possess you, O Yasmin?

YASMIN: Am I not a desert waiting for the rain? Is not my bosom burning for kisses?

HASSAN: Are not your lips love's roses, your cheeks love's lilies, your eyes love's hyacinths?

YASMIN: Ya, Hassan, and my hair the net of love, and my girdle the chain of love that breaks at a lover's touch!

HASSAN: I am drowning in a wave of madness. Let me in, Yasmin; let me in!

YASMIN: Ah, if I could!

HASSAN: Why not?

YASMIN: Ah, if I dared!

HASSAN: What do you fear? It is night, and the street is silent.

YASMIN: Ah, dear Hassan, but I am not alone.

HASSAN (*whispering*): Not alone? Who is there? Your mother?

YASMIN: No! One whom you sent here.

HASSAN: I sent no one.

YASMIN: One of your friends.

HASSAN: A man?

SELIM (*poking his head out of the window*):   Ya, Hassan, Salaam aleikum. I thank you for directing my steps to this rose-strewn bower.

HASSAN (*astonished*):   Selim!

SELIM: Thy servant always.

HASSAN (*wildly*):   Selim!

SELIM: Be advised, O Hassan, go and seek the enchanted egg.

HASSAN: Selim, what do you here?

SELIM: Plunge not the finger of enquiry into the pie of impertinence, O my uncle.

HASSAN: Since when have I become your uncle, Selim, and how did I cease to be your friend?

SELIM: Since when did you aspire to poetry, O Hassan; but I have heard these lines:

> As from the eagle flies the dove
> So friendship from the claw of love.

HASSAN: Love. What love do you mean, scum of the market?

SELIM: This. (*Puts a hand on Yasmin's shoulder.*)

HASSAN: Do not touch her, you dog, do not touch her!

SELIM: Is it a crime to touch Yasmin, my Uncle? Is not her neck a pillar of the marble of Yoonistan. (*Puts his arm round her neck.*)

HASSAN: Torment of death!

YASMIN: Are not my arms like swords of steel, hard and cold, and thirsty for blood? (*Putting her arms round the neck of Selim.*)

HASSAN: Fire of hell!

SELIM: Are not her eyes two sapphires in two pools?

HASSAN: Woe is me! Woe is me!

YASMIN: Are not my lips two rubies drenched in blood? (*Kisses him.*)

HASSAN: God, I shall fall!

SELIM (*his face in Yasmin's bosom*): Could'st thou but see, O my Uncle, the silver hills with their pomegranate groves; or the deep fountain in the swelling plain, or the Ethiopian who waters the roses in the garden, or the great lamp between the columns where the incense of love is burned. How can I thank thee, O my Uncle, for the name and address, and half the old Jew's dinars!

YASMIN: Ah, it is bitter to be a widow and so young!

HASSAN (*putting up his hands to his head*): The fountain, the fountain! O my head, my head!

YASMIN: Be not too rash, my Uncle, or thy hair will come away in thy hands.

HASSAN: If I could but reach your necks with a knife, children of Sheitan!

YASMIN: Buy, O Hassan, no more juice from Jews.

SELIM: Much I fear, O my friend, for thy character in the market. Men will nudge each other and say, 'Behold Hassan, who gave ten dinars for a pint of indigo and water!'

HASSAN: Ah, death!

YASMIN: Look at him! He is drifting like a soul aswoon! Go home, old fellow!

SELIM: Go home, and write poems!

YASMIN: Go home, and cook sweets!

HASSAN: Yasmin! Yasmin! My head!

YASMIN: Begone, or I will cool thy head, thou wearisome old fool!

HASSAN: Yasmin! Yasmin! (*Stands with his arms out-stretched.*)

YASMIN: Take this, my bulbul, to quench thy aspiration. (*Pours a jug of water over him, and slams the shutters to. Hassan does not budge from his position.*)

HASSAN: O thou villainous, unclean dog, Selim. O thou unutterable woman. I will have you both whipped through the city and impaled in the market-place, and your bodies flung to rot on a dung-heap. May you scream in hell for ever. O, my head—my head. For ever. Thou and thy magic and thy Jew. There is blood dripping from the wall. (*Banging on the gate.*) I will break the house in. I will kill you. Ya, Allah, I am splitting in twain. Ya, Allah, I am dying. Oh, Yasmin, so beautiful, so brutal. O, burning bright; you have killed me! Farewell, and the Salaam!

(*Falls under the shadow of the fountain. Silence. A light appears in the next house. Soft music starts; the first light of dawn shines in the sky.*)

(*Enter the Caliph Haroun al Raschid, Jafar, his Vizier, Masrur (a Negro), his executioner; and Ishak, a young man, his poet, all attired as Merchants.*)

CALIPH: Ishak, my heart is heavy, and still the night drags on, and still we wander in the crooked streets, and still we find no entertainment, and still the white moon shines.

ISHAK: O Caliph of Islam, is there not vast entertainment for the wise in the shining of the moon, in the dripping of that fountain, and in the shape of that tall cypress that has leapt the wall to shoot her arrow at the stars?

(*The music which had stopped, recommences.*)

CALIPH: But I hear music, and see lights. Come on,

come on, we will snatch profit from this cursed night even yet, my friends, even at the eleventh hour.

JAFAR: Master, the night is far advanced, and you have not slept. It is a late hour to seek for entertainment.

CALIPH: Jafar, you are as prudent as a shopkeeper.

ISHAK: There lies his merit, Haroun! For he keeps the great shop of state, he sells the revenue of provinces, and buys in the lives of men.

CALIPH: Enough, enough. Call to them, Jafar, and see if they will let us in.

JAFAR: Oh, gentlefolk, in the name of Allah!

VOICE (*from window, the person invisible*): Who calls?

JAFAR: Sir, we are four merchants who came yesterday night from Basra. We lost our way, and have been wandering since midnight in search of our Khan and have not found it. And now a happy chance has taken us to this street.

VOICE: Then you are not of Bagdad?

JAFAR: No, sir, but of Basra.

VOICE: Had you been of Bagdad, you should not have entered for all the gold in the Caliph's coffers.

CALIPH: Then we may enter, being of Basra?

VOICE: If you enter, you will be in my power. And if you annoy me, I will punish you with death. But no one constraineth you to enter. Go in peace, O men of Basra.

CALIPH (*aside*): A rare adventure. (*Aloud*): We take the risk of annoying you, O host of terror, and are now looking for the door.

VOICE: Since when did a door of good reputation open on to this street, my masters? But I will contrive a means for your ascent.

CALIPH: Jafar, I never suspected there was a great house in this poor quarter of the town. We shall make a discovery to-night, O Jafar.

JAFAR: Master, we have been warned of danger!
(A basket comes down.)

CALIPH: Danger? What care I?
(Sits in the basket, and is drawn up.)

JAFAR: Eh, Masrur, I could sleep a little.

MASRUR: You would wake in Paradise if the Caliph heard you, Jafar.
(Masrur waves his sword dexterously near Jafar's neck.)

JAFAR *(as he ascends into the basket, pointing to Masrur's sword)*: The path to Paradise is narrow and shiny, O Masrur!

MASRUR *(with a grim motion of the sword)*: Ya, Jafar, it is a short cut.
(Jafar having ascended, Masrur ascends, and the basket is let down for Ishak.)

ISHAK *(alone)*: Go on thy way without me, Commander of the Faithful. I will follow you no further. Find one more adventure if you will. For me the break of day is adventure enough—and the water splashing in the fountain. Find out, Haroun, the secret of the lights and of the music, of the house that has no door, and the master that will admit no citizen. Drag out the mystery of a man's love or loss, then break your oath and publish his tale to all Bagdad, then fling him gold, and fling him gold, and dream you have made a friend! Those bags of gold you fling, O my generous master, to a mistress for a night, to a poet for a jest, to a beggar for a whim, are they not the revenues of cities, wrung by torture from the poor? But the sighs of your people, Haroun, do not so much as stir the leaves in your palace garden!

And I—I have taken your gold, I, Ishak, who was born on the mountains free of the woods and winds. I have made my home in your palace, and almost forgot it was a prison. And for you I have strung glittering, fulsome verses, a hundred rhyming to one rhyme, ingeniously woven, my disgrace as a poet, my dishonour as a man. And I have forgotten that there are men who dig and sow, and a hut on the hills where I was born.

(*Perceives Hassan.*) Ah, there is a body, here in the the shade. The corpses of the poor are very common in the streets these days. By his clothes this was a common man, a grocer or a baker, his person ill-proportioned and unseemly, but by his forehead not quite a common man.

JAFAR (*from above*):   Ishak, are you coming up?

ISHAK (*shouting back*):   Wait a minute, I will come.

(*To himself*):   What has curved his mouth into that bitter line?

What? a lute? Take my hand, O brother. You loved music too, and you could sing the songs of the people, which are better than mine—the songs I learnt from the mother of my mother. (*Taking the broken lute mechanically.*)   What was that one?

> The Green Boy came from over the mountains,
> Joy of the morning, joy of his heart?

I have forgotten it, and the lute is broken.

(*Resumes Hassan's hand.*)   Ah, brother, your hand is warm and your heart beating, you are not dead. (*Bathing Hassan's forehead with water from the fountain.*)   I shall know after all what has twisted your mouth awry.

CALIPH: Ishak, Ishak, we wait and wait.

ISHAK: May I not be free one hour, to breathe the dawn

alone! Ah! . . . (*Takes Hassan's body and drags it to the basket.*) I come, my master! (*Puts Hassan in the basket.*) There, take my place, brother, and find your destiny. I will be free to-night, free for one dawn upon the hills! (*As Hassan is drawn up in the basket, Ishak walks rapidly away.*)

CURTAIN

SCENE 3

SCENE: *A great room. To the left three arches lead out on to a balcony where the personages Caliph, Jafar and Host are collected. The interior of the room is blazing with lights, but empty. The architecture of the room is curious on account of the wide, low arches which cut off a square in the centre. The furniture of the room is in rich, rather vulgar Oriental taste.*

CALIPH: Ishak, Ishak, we are waiting and waiting.

JAFAR: Ishak! Ishak! Perhaps he is faint.

CALIPH: Faint! Let him preserve his fainting to eleven tomorrow. Am I to be kept waiting like a Jew in a court of justice, I the Master . . .

JAFAR (*quickly*):   We are not in Basra, Sir. But see, the rope has tightened. (To MASRUR):   Haul, thou whose soul is white.

RAFI (*Host, helping with ropes to Caliph who stands idle*): God restore to you the use of your arms, my brother from Basra.
        (*Hassan rolls out of the basket, filthy and inanimate.*)
        Yallah, Yallah, on what dunghill did this fowl die?

JAFAR (*astonished*):   This is not our companion.

CALIPH: Our friend has played a trick on us—may Allah separate him from salvation!—and sent up this body in place of himself. Come, let us tip it out into the street.

RAFI (*feeling Hassan's pulse*):   Wait; this man is by no means dead, and the mill of his heart still grinds the flour of life. Ho, Alder!

19

(*Enter Alder, a young and pretty page.*)

ALDER: At his master's service.

RAFI: Ho, Willow!

WILLOW (*younger still*):   At his lord's order.

RAFI: Juniper!

JUNIPER: At his Pasha's command.

RAFI: Tamarisk!

TAMARISK (*a little boy with a squeaky voice*):   At his Sublimity's feet.

CALIPH (*aside to Jafar*):   Truly, this is charming: an illustrious example of decorum and good taste.

RAFI: Transform this into a man, my slaves, and bring him back to us.

ALDER: We hear,

WILLOW: We honour,

JUNIPER: We tremble,

TAMARISK: and obey.

CALIPH (*entering the great room of the house*):   Thy house is of grand proportions and eccentric architecture, my Host; it is astonishing that such a house should look out on to so mean a street.

RAFI: It is an old house wherein the Manichees (the devil roast all heretics!) once held their meetings before they were all flayed alive. It is called the House of the Moving Walls.

CALIPH: Why such a name?

RAFI: I cannot tell you and you must not ask. Ho, music! Ho, dancers! (*Claps his hands.*)

   (*Music plays. The Host enters the room and motions his Guests to be seated in silence.*)

CALIPH: Verily, after this prelude, and in this splendid palace, we shall see dancing women worthy of Paradise.

20

JAFAR: God grant it, Master.

CALIPH (*to Jafar*):   Hush, I hear the pattering of feet. The wine of anticipation is dancing through my veins. O Jafar, what incomparable houris will charm our eyes to-night? What rosy breasts, what silver shoulders, what shapely legs, what jasmine arms!

(*In good order, marching to the music, there enter the most awful selection of Eastern Beggars the eye could imagine, or the tongue describe. They are headed by their Chief, a rather fine fellow, in indescribable tatters. He leads the Chorus with a song, half intoned in the Oriental style.*)

LEADER: Fathers of two feet, advance,
          Dot and go ones, hop along,
          Two feet missing need not dance,
          But will join us in the song.

CHORUS OF CULS-DE-JATTE:
          But will join you in the song.

LEADER: Show your most revolting scar;
          People never weary of it.
          The more nauseous you are—
          More their pity and your profit.

CHORUS: And your profit, profit, profit.

LEADER: Cracked of lip and gapped of tooth,
          Apoplectic, maim or mad,
          Blind of one eye, blind of both,
          Up, the beggars of Bagdad.

CHORUS: Up, the beggars of Bagdad.

LEADER: There's a cellar, I am told,
          Where a little lamp is lit,
          And that cellar's full of gold,
          Sacks and sacks and sacks of it.

CHORUS (*hoarsely*):
>> Sacks and sacks and sacks of it,
>> Stacks and stacks and stacks of it.
>> Open eyes and stiffen backs,
>> There are sacks and sacks and sacks;
>> And gold for him who lacks of it.

(*The Host lifts his hand. The Beggars all fall flat on their
faces. Dance music.*)

(*Enter right, a Band of fair, left, a Band of dusky, beauties.*)

THE DANCING GIRLS:
>> Daughters of delight, advance,
>> Petals, petals, drift along;
>> Cypress, tremble! Firefly, dance!
>> Nightingale, your song, your song!

THE FAIR: We are pale

THE DARK: as dawn, with roses,
>> O the roses, O desire!
>> We are dark,

THE FAIR (*curtsying*): but as the twilight
>> Shooting all the sky with fire.

CHORUS: Daughters of delight, advance.
>> Petals, petals, drift along,
>> Cypress tremble! Firefly, dance!
>> Nightingale, your song, your song!

(*They surround the Beggars, dancing, and point at them.*)

LEADER OF THE FAIR:
>> From what base tavern, of what street
>> Were dragged these dogs, that foul our feet?

LEADER OF THE DARK:
>> O sisters, fly, we shall be hurt:
>> (*The Leader of the Beggars catches her.*)
>> Leave go my ankle, son of dirt.

LEADER OF THE BEGGARS:

> Lady, if the dirt should gleam,
>> Feel, but do not show surprise:
> Things that happen here would seem

(*Rises to his feet, his rags drop off, and he shines in gold.*)
>> Paradox in Paradise.

(*The infirmities and rags of the whole Band disappear as if by magic, as they rise and shout in Chorus.*)

CHORUS: Paradox in Paradise.

> (*Rafi raises his hand. All stand at attention.*)

VOICES: Hush, the King speaks
>> The King of the Beggars.
>> The King.

LEADER OF THE BEGGARS:

> The King of the Beggars, the Caliph of the Faithless, the Peacock of the Silver Path, the Master of Bagdad!
> (*The Ballet line the room behind the arches.*)

JAFAR (*aside, astonished*):   King of the Beggars?

MASRUR (*aside, astonished*):   Master of Bagdad?

CALIPH (*aside, astonished*):   Caliph of the Faithless? Allah kerim, this is a jest indeed!

RAFI (*throwing off his outer garment and discovering himself superbly dressed in a golden armour*):   Subjects and Guests. Now that the night before our day is ending, and the Wolf's Tail is already brushing the eastern sky, now our plot is ready, our conspiracy established, our victory imminent. Shall I say, be brave? You are lions. Be cunning? You are serpents. Be bloody? You are wolves.

Listen, O, Beggars! How loud they snore, those swine whose nostrils we shall slit to-day! Copper they flung to us, and steel we shall give them back; good steel of Damascus' that digs a narrow hole and deep.

But as for the Peacock of Peacocks, that sack of debauch, that Caliph, alive in his coffin, I and none other will nail him down, with his eyes staring into mine. His gardens, fountains, summer-houses, and palaces; his horses, mules, camels, and elephants, his statues of Yoonistan, and his wines of Ferangistan, his eunuchs of Egypt, and his carpets of Bokhara, and his great sealed boxes bursting with unbeaten gold, all this and all his women, his chosen flower-like women, are yours for lust and loot and lechery, my children—all save her you dare not touch, the lady of the Red Pavilion, she is mine, and she shall sit unveiled with me on the throne of all the Caliphs . . . and when you see us sitting on that throne together, then you shall cry . . .

THE BEGGARS (*taking up with a shout*): The Caliph is dead! The Caliphate is over! Long live the King!

JAFAR (*in indignation*): These words are not holy, even in jest.

RAFI: O guests of an hour, I pray you put the tongue of discretion into the cheek of propriety.

JAFAR: Propriety! The host's obligations are greater than the guests. It is not good taste to speak thus before the invited.

RAFI: The self-invited, says the poet, must not be surprised.

JAFAR: Sir, I pray you, no more of this, be it jest or earnest. It will soon be morning: we must away: we have pressing business: our clients await us.

RAFI: Before dawn, O fortunate and much frequented merchants? Come, no more word of departure at your peril.

MASRUR (*drawing his sword*):   Dost thou dare threaten us, Bismillah!

RAFI: Truly, O most disgusting negro, comprehension and thou have been separated since thy youth. Shall I then drop the needle of insinuation and pick up the club of statement? Shall I tell you three guests of mine, with the plainness of plainness and the openness of plainness, that if you offer one threat more, propose one evasion more, or ask one question more, I will thrash your lives head downwards from your feet!

(*Enter Hassan finely dressed, ushered in by the Four Boys through the rows of Dancers.*)

HASSAN (*lamenting*):   Eywallah, eywallah, eywah, eywah, Mashallah! Istagfurallah!

RAFI: Why, here is the fourth guest!

ALDER: We have washed him: he needed it.

WILLOW: Combed him: it was necessary.

JUNIPER: Scented him: it was our duty.

TAMARISK: Clothed him: it was our delight.

HASSAN (*as before*):   Eywallah! Yallah Akbar! Yallah kerim! Istagfurallah! Eywallah! Hassan is ended! Hassan is no more! He is dead! He is buried! He is a bone! Yallah kerim!

RAFI: Eywah Hassan, if that is your name, have my boys not treated you well?

HASSAN: Oh, Master, have mercy. Who are these terrible men?

RAFI: Beggars of Bagdad! Ten thousand more await my signal in the streets. In a few minutes they will surprise the drowsy Palace Guards, sack Bagdad, kill the Caliph and make me King.

HASSAN: Alas! (*stupefied.*) What has become of me this

night! Just now I was in Hell, with all the fountains raining fire and blood.

RAFI: Come, Hassan, you are only just in time; the cold dawn which ends the revellers' dark day will soon be uncurtaining the blue. One bowl to pledge me victory. At least you shall say this of your host—he gave us splendid wine.

(*The Four Slaves hand round the bowl; the Caliph refuses.*)

(*To Caliph*): Sir, you do not drink.

CALIPH: I obey the Prophet.

RAFI: The Prophet should have been a Syrian like this vintage.

JAFAR: Come, host! Never will I refuse the bowl from Pasha, thief or Christian.

MASRUR: Host, may I drink your blood as I drink your wine. (*Drinks.*)

RAFI (*sarcastically*): Ye are jolly fellows after all and amiably disposed. (*Drinks.*) I thank you, negro, I drink to yours. Drink thou, too, O corpse from the basket.

HASSAN: I drink to forget a woman, but will this little cup suffice?

RAFI: Nor ten, nor ten thousand little cups like these, if you have loved. To-night I shall fill my bowl of oblivion with the blood of the Caliph of Bagdad. Brother, will that great cup suffice?

HASSAN (*in terror*): Call me not brother, thou savage man, who dost dare talk of shedding the holiest blood in Islam!

RAFI: When high office is polluted, when the holy is unholy, when justice is a lie, when the people are starved, and the great fools of the world in high office, then dares a man so talk.

CALIPH: Also when one has a vengeance to wreak on the

26

Caliph and a claim on a lady of his household.

MASRUR: Why do you want to nail him in his coffin alive?

JAFAR: Do you covet his riches, you who clothe your beggars in cloth of gold?

RAFI: I will brand the text of your questions on your naked backs if you ask me more.

(*After hesitation.*) Yet, what harm can it do, if for my own sake, to relieve the heaviness of my heart, I tell you something of my story?

My name is Rafi. I come from the hills beyond Mosul, where the men walk free and the women go unveiled. There I was betrothed to Pervaneh, a woman beautiful and wise. But the very day before our marriage the Governor of Mosul remembered my country and invaded it with a thousand men. And they caught Pervaneh walking alone among the pine woods and carried her away. When I heard this I leapt on my horse and followed them to Mosul. There I found she had already been sent with a raft full of slaves down the Tigris to Bagdad. Whereupon I hired six men with shining muscles to row me there. We arrived at Bagdad at the end of the third night's rowing at the grey of dawn. I sprang out of the raft like a tiger, and ran like a madman through the streets, crying 'The Slave Market! Tell me the way, O ye citizens! The Slave Market, O the Slave Market!'

And suddenly turning a corner I came upon the market, which was like a garden full of girls in splendid clothes grouped in groups like flowers in garden beds; and some like lilies, naked. I ran round the market to find Pervaneh, and behold there she stood; she who had never worn a veil before, the only veiled woman in all the market, for she had sworn to bite off her lips if her master would not veil her: but I knew her by the beauty of her hands. I cried: 'O dealer, the veiled woman for a thousand dinars!' And the dealer laughed in the way of dealers at the presumption of my offer and accepted. Pervaneh lifted her veil and sang for joy, and all the slave girls clapped their hands.

But at that moment there entered the market a negro eunuch. And all the dealers and the slaves bowed low before him. Coming to my dealer, he cried: 'Why dost thou sell slaves before the Caliph has made his choice?'

Then turning to Pervaneh, he said, 'Go back to thy place.' And I cried, 'She is my purchase.' But the eunuch said, 'Hold thy peace; I take her for the Caliph.' And Pervaneh cried in the speech of my country, as they carried her away: 'I will die, but I will not be defiled: rescue me alive or dead, soon or late, and avenge me on this Caliph!'

That is my story, and for this reason I will nail the Caliph down in his coffin, bound and living and with open eyes.

CALIPH (*in horror*): The devil!

MASRUR: Is that all the story?

JAFAR: Will you tear up Islam for the honour of a girl?

CALIPH (*in fury*): And set your paramour in scale against the Prophet's chosen?

RAFI: What's the Prophet or the chosen of the Prophet to the destruction of that soul, the dishonour of that body? And shall I not avenge my wrong with the vengeance of a thousand others. With me shall be avenged those naked beggars who shiver in the streets at night.

JAFAR: God will frustrate thee, madman!

RAFI: If He will. Farewell, my guests. I go to avenge
Pervaneh, and to wash Bagdad in blood. Bide my
return. You will be as safe here as in an iron
cage.

CALIPH (*rushing to intercept him*):   By the thick smoke of
Hell's Pit and the Ghouls that eat men's flesh, you shall
not go, and we shall not stay.

RAFI: Look twice before you touch me!

(*He leaps behind the archway. The Beggars and the Women are
now lined close to the wall of the room and the Guests are
isolated in the centre. From behind every pillar appears an
Archer with bow drawn taut directed on the startled
Guests.*)

(*To the Guests*):   Did not someone ask me why this
house was called the House of the Moving Walls?

CALIPH: I did!

(*Sheets of iron fall with a crash covering the apertures of the
arches. The Four Guests are completely walled in.*)

RAFI, BEGGARS AND WOMEN (*from behind the iron partitions
with a shout*):   Answered!

(*The Beggars tramp out to martial music.*)

CHORUS OF BEGGARS AND DANCING GIRLS:

> To-day the fools who catch a cold in summer
>   Will fly for winter in the windy moon.
> To-day the little rills of shining water
>   Will catch the fire of morning oversoon.
> To-day the state musicians and court poets
>   Will set new verses to a special tune.
> To-day Haroun, the much-detested Caliph
>   Will find his Caliphate inopportune.

JAFAR (*listening at the wall*): They have all left the room. At least we are alone. Let us shout, they may hear us from the street.

MASRUR (*banging on the wall*): Eywah! Help, help, men of Bagdad! The Caliph is in danger! The Caliph is in prison! . . . Come up and save the Caliph, the Master of Men, the Shaker of the World! . . .

(*Silence.*)

JAFAR: I had forgotten the height of this room above the street: and on either side stretches the empty garden of this house!

(*The Calph, Jafar and Masrur rush round as though trying to find a way out of their prison, and banging on the iron walls. Hassan takes his seat on the carpet.*)

CALIPH: Allah! and this room is a box within a box like a Chinese toy. And that man will surprise my soldiers in the chill of dawn, and sack my palace and burn Bagdad. He will discover my identity and bury me alive!

JAFAR: Alas, Master! What shall we do?

CALIPH: Thou dog! Thou dirt! Thou dunghill! Thou dustheap! Did I make thee Vizier to ask counsel or to give it? Find out what we shall do. Thou hast let me fall into a trap, and now dost quiver and quake and shiver and shake like a tub of whey on the back of a restive camel: my kingdom is reduced from twelve provinces to twelve square cubits: my subjects from thirty millions unto three, but, Bismillah! one of my subjects is the Executioner, and Mashallah! another one merits execution: and Inshallah! if thy head doth not immediately devise a practicable scheme of escape it shall dive off thy shoulders and swim across the floor.

JAFAR: What shall happen, shall happen. But here is one who is occupied in meditation, and is aloof from the circumstances of the moment: let us invite him to Council.

CALIPH: Ho, thou Hassan! What occupies thy spirit?

HASSAN: I am examining the square of carpet. It is of cheap manufacture, inferior dye and unpleasant pattern.

CALIPH: Art thou a carpet dealer?

HASSAN: No, sir, I am a confectioner.

CALIPH: And I am the Caliph.

HASSAN: As my heart surmised, O Commander of the Faithful! (*Performs the ceremonies prescribed.*)

CALIPH: Canst thou give me one gleam of hope of salvation, Hassan, the Confectioner? If not, Masrur shall cut the knot of existence for all of us. I dare not fall into that man's hands alive.

HASSAN: What of the man who put me in the basket?

CALIPH: No good—no good. I would rather depend on the mercy of Rafi than on the whim of Ishak. Masrur, unsheathe. There is no hope.

HASSAN: Thy pardon on thy servant: Poets have said in light is Hope and in a ray Salvation.
(*Points to crack between bottom of the iron wall and floor, towards the balcony.*)

CALIPH: By the seven lakes of Hell, we are not mice!

HASSAN: A mouse could not pass. But what, O Master, of a message?

CALIPH: A message?

HASSAN: Written out black on paper, and dropped into the street.

CALIPH: Saved! Saved! O, Glory of the sunshine! O, splendour of the world! Ho, Jafar, thou art a fool to this man! Take out thy pen and write. Warn the Captain of the Soldiers. Warn the Police. Describe our position. Offer the Government of Three Provinces to the man who picks up the paper. Write for the Salvation of Bagdad; write for the safety of Islam! O Hassan, the Confectioner, if we are rescued I will fill thy mouth with gold!

(*Jafar having written on a long roll of paper, they thrust it in the crack.*)

HASSAN: No: at the corner here, where there is no balcony and the wall drops straight into the street.

(*Masrur pokes out the paper with his sword.*)

CALIPH: And now how shall we employ the time of waiting for our deliverance?

JAFAR: I shall meditate upon the mutability of human affairs.

MASRUR: And I shall sharpen my sword upon my thigh.

HASSAN: And I shall study the reasons of the excessive ugliness of the pattern of this carpet.

CALIPH: Hassan, I will join thee: thou art a man of taste!

SCENE 4

SCENE: *Again the street outside the house—the Street of the Fountain, with the balcony of Rafi and the balcony of Yasmin opposite. Cold light before dawn.*

On the steps of the Fountain, two tired Mendicants asleep. One slowly rubs his eyes and looks round him. A paper comes floating down. One tired Man lazily catches it.

FIRST LOITERER: Here comes a new chapter of the Koran falling down from Heaven.

SECOND LOITERER: Is it written, Abdu?

ABDU: It is written, Ali.

ALI: Read what is written, Abdu.

ABDU: I cannot read. Am I a schoolmaster?

(*Folds paper, puts it in his belt, and prepares to sleep again. Several interesting Orientals pass by.*)

ALI: Abdu!

ABDU: I sleep.

ALI: I can read: give me the paper.

ABDU: I am asleep: get up and take it from my belt if you want it, Ya Ali, I am heavy with great sleep, like a tortoise in November.

ALI: Ya Abdu, I am too languishing to move. It is a paper and it is written. It does not matter. To-morrow or the next day it will be read.

ABDU: To-morrow or the next day I shall wake and pass it to you.

(*Interval: more interesting Orientals go by.*)

ALI (*with sudden inspiration*):   Blow me the paper, Abdu.

33

ABDU: Alas, Allah sent thee to trouble the world!
(*Abdu blows the paper over. Ali with infinite difficulty spells it out, murmuring:*)

ALI: Ha, alif, alif re wow wow 'ain Jeem—ah, ye blessed ones in Paradise, is it thus ye write a Jeem? Nun—but art thou a nun, O letter, or a drunkard's Qaf? Verily an ape has written this with his tail: I have the second line. (*With a start.*) Ho, Abdu, whence came this? Stop your snore! Answer me.

ABDU: From the sky: how do I know?

ALI: Let me look at the sky. (*Rolls on his back and stares upward.*) I tell you, Abdu, a mighty joker has flung this from the balcony.

ABDU: Allah plague him and his pen and thee! Is there no peace in the world?

ALI: Here it is written, and do thou listen, O Abdu, for this is the strangest of the strange writings that are strange: 'Whoever findeth this paper, know that the Caliph is in the house above, a prisoner, and his friends prisoners, and in the extremity of danger, he and they, with all Bagdad. Let the rescue be swift and sudden, but above all secret. The iron walls must be lifted from beneath. Go quick to the Guard, O fortunate discoverer, warn them to protect the palace against the Beggars of Bagdad, and thou shalt be made Governor of Three Provinces. Signed, Jafar, the Vizier.' (*Bursting into laughter.*) Three Provinces, well I know their Three Provinces! (*In a lower voice.*) And I tell you, Abdu, what if the Caliph were in the house and his friends? What if this were true?

ABDU: May the great gripes settle on thee and on the Caliph and the mother of the Caliph. Who are you to

34

rescue the Caliph and prevent me from sleeping?

ALI: True, one should never meddle in politics. Ya, Jehannum, the Police!

(Chief of Police with Ishak.)

ISHAK: I tell you, I do not know precisely where I left them. It was night. It may have been this balcony or that, but there are a thousand balconies. It was above a fountain, but there are a million fountains. I tell you they always come back. Have you not already had twenty such scares as these for the safety of the Caliph?

CHIEF OF POLICE: Never and on no preceding occasion has his exalted name been so long delayed in his return to the palace. The day is dawning.

ISHAK: I tell you, if you do find him you will get no thanks, O man of arms. Will you dare to unstick the Ruler of the Moslem World from the embrace of his latest slave girl or dash the cup of pleasure from his reluctant hand?

CHIEF OF POLICE: I tell you, if you do not find him, O man of letters, I will have you impaled upon a monstrous pen.

(Seizes him.)

ISHAK: Thou beastly, blood-drinking brute and bloated bully, take off thy stable-reeking hands.

CHIEF OF POLICE: Yallah, these poets. They talk in rhyme.

ALI *(who has risen and salaamed, advancing)*: I pray you, Sirs, . . .

CHIEF OF POLICE: O thou maggot! Darest thou address us?

ALI: I pray you only regard . . .

CHIEF OF POLICE: I pray you only remove, or I will split you from the top.

ISHAK: Do you not see that he has a paper, and that his manners are superior to yours, O Captain of Police. Let me look at thy paper. . . . Ah—ah. Whence came this, O virtuous wanderer?

ALI: From that balcony, may thy slave be forgiven!

CHIEF OF POLICE: This is a very important clue. Let us break in the door.

ISHAK: There is no door. But first of all send word to the Palace Guard.

CHIEF OF POLICE (*to a policeman*): Ali. (*To the other Ali, who runs and says:* Excellence, I hear and obey.) Not thou, fool. Did Allah make the name Ali for thee alone? Who are thou that I should address thee? Are there not ten thousand Alis in Bagdad, and wilt thou lift up thy head, O worm, when I say Ali? (*To policeman*): Here is my ring. Take this paper, and run with all thy might and show it to the Captain of the Palace guard.

POLICEMAN: I hear and obey. (*Starts off.*)

ISHAK (*stopping him*): Wait!

CHIEF OF POLICE: What right have you to stop my man, you bastard son of a quill-bearing barn-fowl?

ISHAK: Since when had a bludgeoning policeman the practical good sense of a thought-breathing poet? Tell them, to send men with levers and ladders.

CHIEF OF POLICE: Good! Run, slave.

ISHAK: You now!

ALI: Master?

ISHAK: How long is it since any paper was thrown from the balcony?

ALI: How do I know time? The time to go to market and buy a melon.

CHIEF OF POLICE: By the great pit of torment, this swine-faced has had the paper a good hour! By the red blaze of damnation, thou maggot, why didst thou not run with this at once to the Palace Guard, worm?

ALI: I was afraid, and I thought it was a jest.

CHIEF OF POLICE: A jest! Rivers of blood, a jest! The life of the Caliph of Bagdad, a jest! I will teach thee jesting. I will teach thee fear. Ho, Mahmud, Zia, Rustem, down with his head and up with his heels.

ALI (*as his feet are looped into the pole to receive the bastinado*): Ya Abdu, you had the letter first, it is yours. Will you not claim it and the reward? Alas, that the Governor of Three Provinces should be treated thus!

ABDU: Do I meedle in politics? Hit him hard, O Executioner, for he is a great disturber of peaceful citizens. But as for me, I will make my way a little further on. (*Exit.*)

(*The Policemen proceed with their work, but stop on entrance of Captain of the Military with Soldiers. Yasmin appears on the balcony of her house.*)

YASMIN: Look, look, Selim! there's a man being beaten.

SELIM: Come in quick! this is a riot or some trouble; come in quick, and shut the shutters fast.

YASMIN: You are a valiant protection indeed for frail-as-a-rose ladies in danger's hour!

(*They remain at the window.*)

CAPTAIN OF MILITARY (*to Chief of Police*): Sir.

CHIEF OF POLICE: Sir.

CAPTAIN OF MILITARY (*saluting*): Captain of the Victorious Army, at your service!

CHIEF OF POLICE (*saluting*): Chief of the August Police, at yours.

37

CAPTAIN OF MILITARY (*bowing*): I am honoured.

CHIEF OF POLICE (*bowing*): I am overwhelmed.

ISHAK: Come, Sirs, brush away, I implore you, the cobwebs of ceremony with the broom of expedition.

CHIEF OF POLICE: Sir, when men of action meet, the place of the man of letters is inside his pen-case.

CAPTAIN OF MILITARY: A moment! Ere we proceed, Chief of Police, may I ask why this man is undergoing punishment?

CHIEF OF POLICE: Since your excellency deigns to enquire, for urgent reasons of police.

CAPTAIN OF MILITARY: They must have been very urgent indeed before you would permit such an inopportune disturbance outside the very house where our Lord the Caliph is imprisoned. You have seriously impaired our chances of a speedy and effective rescue.

CHIEF OF POLICE (*drawing his sword and whirling it about*): Thou melon head, thou dung pig, thou brother of disaster, get thee hence with thy knock-kneed band of fatherless brigands.

CAPTAIN OF MILITARY: Out with thy sword, thou big-bellied snatcher up of burglars, thou manacler of little boys, thou terror of the peaceful market. I will teach thee to insult the slaughterers of the infidel host.

ISHAK (*intercepting the Combatants*): Is this a time for indecent brawling? Quick, where are the ladders?

A SOLDIER (*pompously*): In the rear, Sir, in the rear.

(*The ladders are brought along.*)

CHIEF OF POLICE (*to Policemen*): Place a ladder.

CAPTAIN OF MILITARY (*to Soldiers*): Place a ladder.

CHIEF OF POLICE: The rescue of the Caliph is obviously and exclusively the duty of the Police.

CAPTAIN OF MILITARY: The safety of the Celestial One is entirely the concern of his military warriors.

(*Each goes up his ladder at the same time: bang at the iron wall and are answered: shout for levers which are procured. The iron wall is lifted up, and the Caliph and the Rest disclosed seated peaceably awaiting their deliverance, the lamp still burning.*)

CHIEF OF POLICE: My royal master!

CAPTAIN OF MILITARY: August Lord.

CHIEF AND CAPTAIN (*together*): I have saved thee, Master.
(*Each attempts to seize the Caliph.*)

CHIEF OF POLICE: Honourable Police! . . .

CAPTAIN OF MILITARY: Honourable Military! . . .

CHIEF OF POLICE: It has been the high privilege of this grovelling slave to rescue the Lamp of the World. I shall carry him down.

CAPTAIN OF MILITARY: Permit me to observe, O fire-spitting Battle Cleaver, that I was first up this ladder, and that it is I who have the prior claim.

(*Masrur pushes them aside, and assists the Caliph down the ladder. Jafar and Hassan follow. Shouts of 'Long live the Caliph' from all the people gathered in the street. The Soldiers salute. The Caliph raises his hand. Silence.*)

CALIPH: Is my Palace safe?

MASRUR: O Lord and Master, we pray so.

CALIPH: And my people?

JAFAR: Around thee, O Lord and Master.

YASMIN (*from her balcony*): By the Prophet, here is Hassan with the Caliph!

CALIPH: Are we all saved?

MASRUR: All, by the providence of Allah.

JAFAR: And the wisdom of Hassan.

CALIPH: And the Guard warned?

CAPTAIN OF MILITARY: All warned and at their posts, my Lord.

CALIPH: Allah, deliver our enemies into their hands! Let Hassan come before me.

HASSAN (*prostrating himself*):   Master!

CALIPH (*raising him*):   Rise, Hassan. This Hassan, yester-day a stranger, has to-night by his skill and invention, saved my life and rescued this city from a greater peril than my death.

CROWD: May it be far!

CALIPH: Therefore here and now, in the presence of all, I nominate Hassan to my court, to hold rank among my subjects second to none save to Jafar, my Grand Vizier.

YASMIN (*who has been at her balcony with Selim*):   O Allah!

CROWD: Honour to Hassan! Honour to Hassan!

HASSAN: Master, I sold confectionery in the market.

JAFAR: Thou shalt now confection the sweets of prosperity.

ISHAK (*to Hassan*):   Why, Hassan! You are the man with the broken lute.

CALIPH: Is that the voice of Ishak?

ISHAK: It is the voice of Ishak that has often sung to you.

CALIPH: Why did you abandon me, Ishak, and flee into the night?

ISHAK: I was weary of you, Haroun-al-Raschid.

CALIPH: And if I weary of you?

ISHAK: You will weary of me one day or another, and you will have me slain.

CALIPH: And what of this day that dawns.

ISHAK: Dawn is the hour when most men die.

CALIPH: Your death is granted you, Ishak; you have but
to kneel.

(*A red glow on the horizon.*)

ISHAK (*as he kneels calmly*):   Why have they pinned the
carpet of execution on the sky?

MASRUR: It is the Caliph's dawn.

JAFAR: Thy dawn, O Master!

ISHAK: Thy dawn O Master of the World, thy dawn;
The hour the lilies open on the lawn,
The hour the grey wings pass beyond the moun-
tains,
The hour of silence, when we hear the fountains,
The hour that dreams are brighter and winds
colder,
The hour that young love wakes on a white
shoulder,
O Master of the World, the Persian Dawn.

[*Not spoken in performance.*]

That hour, O Master, shall be bright for thee:
Thy merchants chase the morning down the sea,
The braves who fight thy war unsheathe the sabre,
The slaves who work thy mines are lashed to labour,
For thee the waggons of the world are drawn—
The ebony of night, the red of dawn!

CALIPH: Sheathe your sword, Masrur! Would you kill
my friend?

MASRUR: I hear and obey.

CALIPH: I must go swiftly to my palace. But to you,
Ishak, I leave the care of this man you sent up to me in
the basket. Teach him the ceremonies and regulations.
Is my chair ready?

BEARERS: Ready, Lord and Master.

41

(*Exit the Caliph in chair, and Jafar and Crowd; Ishak signs to those who would kiss Hassan's feet to leave him.*)

YASMIN (*on balcony opposite. Giving Selim a great clout on the ear*): Go, leave my sight, you fool. I shall burst with fury. You made me insult Hassan, and now he is going to court.

SELIM (*astonished*): Eh, Yasmin, Yasmin, how could I know?

ISHAK: Ah, Bismillah, I had not forgotten you, O man with the broken lute.

HASSAN: Was it here? Is that the balcony? Who are you? Why do you mock me? What do you know?

ISHAK: Quietly, friend, quietly, your head is weak with joy.

HASSAN: With joy? Do I know what is true or false? Do I know if the Caliph is the Caliph? And if the Caliph is the Caliph may he not mock me too? What is joy? Let me look at that balcony for joy. I dare not look, I fear she is there. Ah, it is she!

(*Yasmin takes the rose from her hair and flings it at Hassan, then retires within.*)

ISHAK: Are you fortunate in love as well as in life, O Hassan? But come away. This conduct ill beseems a minister of state; you are not unobserved.

HASSAN: I am coming. The rose is poisoned.

ISHAK: O friend, is this talk for the ardent lover? Last night, I found you lying like a filthy corpse beneath this window, but I knew by your lute and your countenance that you were a poet, like myself.

HASSAN: A poet? I? I am a confectioner. And what is your name?

ISHAK: Ishak is my name.

HASSAN: You are Ishak, the glorious singer of Islam? The splendour of the Caliphate, that Ishak?

ISHAK: I am Ishak, that Ishak, the poet, a man of no repute.

HASSAN: And you will be my friend?

ISHAK: I am your friend, Hassan.

HASSAN: Then consider this rose. This rose is more bitter than colocynth. For look you, friend, had she not flung this rose, I would have said she hated me and loved another; it is well. She had the right to hate and love. She could hate and she could love. But now, ah, tell me, you who seem to be a friend, are all you poets liars?

ISHAK: Ya, Hassan, but we tell excellent lies.

HASSAN: Why do you say that beauty has a meaning? Why do you not say that beauty is as hollow as a drum? Why do you not say it is sold?

ISHAK: All this disillusionment because a fair lady flung you a rose!

HASSAN: Last night I baked sugar and she flung me water: this morning I bake gold and she flings me a rose. Empty, empty, I tell you, friend, all the blue sky!

ISHAK: Come, forget her and come away. I will instruct you in the pleasures of the court.

HASSAN: Forget, forget? O rose of morning and O rose of evening, vainly for me shall you fade on domes of ebony or azure. This rose has faded, and this rose is bitter, and this rose is nothing but the world.

CURTAIN

ACT II

SCENE 1

SCENE: *A small pavilion set within the garden of the Caliph's palace. The Caliph: Hassan in fine rainment, a sword of honour at his side.*

CALIPH: Yes, what the chief Eunuch told you is all true, my Hassan. Our late host, the King of the Beggars, was captured hiding in the gutter of his roof. But whether by my Chief of Police or by my Captain of Military, Allah knows, for they dispute like cats. This day I shall judge him and his crew in full Divan. And in the Divan shalt thou appear, O Hassan, clothed in thy robe of ceremony, and seated on my right hand.

HASSAN: Alas, O Serene Splendour, thy servant is a man of humble origin and limited desires. I am not one to strut among courtiers in robes of state. Sir, excuse me from these things. But at evening, when God flings roses through the sky, call me then to some calm pavilion, and let us hear Ishak play and let us hear Ishak sing, till you forget you are Lord of all the World, and I forget that I am a baseborn tradesman; till we discover the speech of things that have no life, and know what the clods of earth are saying to the roots of the garden trees.

CALIPH: Have no fear. In this case you are a witness and must be present at my Divan, be it but for this once only. And you shall call me Emir of the Faithful, Redresser of

44

Wrong, the Shadow of God on Earth, and Peacock of the World. But in this garden you are Hassan, and I am your friend Haroun, and you must address me as a friend, a friend.

HASSAN: Master, I find thy friendship like thy palace, endowed with all the charm of beauty and the magic of surprise.

CALIPH: Truly, Hassan, never have I seen a man like you for beauty. When you tread on a carpet, you drop your eyes to earth to catch the pattern and when you hear a poem, you raise your eyes to heaven to hear the tune. When did you learn poetry, Hassan of my heart?

HASSAN: In that great school, the Market of Bagdad. For thee, Master of the World, poetry is a princely diversion but for us it is a deliverance from Hell. Allah made poetry a cheap thing to buy and a simple thing to understand. He gave men dreams by night that they might learn to dream by day. Men who work hard have special need of dreams. All the town of Bagdad is passionate for poetry, O Master. Dost thou not know what great crowds gather to hear the epic of Antari sung in the streets at evening. I have seen cobblers weep and butchers bury their great faces in their hands!

CALIPH: By Eblis and the powers of Hell, should I not know this, and know that therein lies the secret of the strength of Islam? In poems and in tales alone shall live the eternal memory of this city when I am dust and thou art dust. Ah, if there shall ever arise a nation whose people have forgotten poetry or whose poets have forgotten the people, though they mine a league into earth or mount to the stars on wings—what of them?

HASSAN: They will be a dark patch upon the world.

CALIPH: Well said! By your luck you have saved the life of the Caliph, O Hassan; but by your conversation you have won the friendship of Haroun. At what are you gazing as if enchanted?

HASSAN: The beautiful fountain, with the silver dolphin and the naked boy.

CALIPH: A Greek of Constantinople made it, who came travelling hither in the days of my father, the Caliph El Mahdi (may earth be gentle to his body and Paradise refreshing to his soul!). He showed this fountain to my father, who asked the Greek if he could make more as fine. 'A hundred,' replied the delighted infidel. Whereupon my father cried, 'Impale this pig.' Which having been done, this fountain remains the loveliest in the world.

HASSAN (*with anguish*):   O Fountain, dost thou never run with blood?

CALIPH: Why, what is the matter, Hassan?

HASSAN: You have told a tale of death and tyranny, O Master of the World.

CALIPH (*in a sudden and towering rage*):   Do you accuse my father of tyranny, O fellow, for slaying a filthy Christian?

HASSAN (*prostrating himself*):   I meant no offence. My life is at your feet. But you bade me talk to you as a friend.

CALIPH: Not Ishak, not Ishak himself, who has been my friend for years would dare address me thus. (*Bursting into laughter.*) Rise, Hassan. Thy impudence hath a monstrous beauty, like the hindquarters of an elephant.

HASSAN: Forgive me, forgive me. I will forget the fountain.

CALIPH: I forgive you with all my heart, but, I advise you, keep to your poetry and carpets, and never leave the Garden of Art for the Palace of Action. Trouble not your head with the tyranny of Princes, or you may catch a cold therein from the Wind of Complication.

HASSAN (*dolefully*): I hear and obey.

CALIPH: Forget it now; set your mind on pleasant things. Have you noticed this little pavilion where we have talked so long? This is your little house, good Hassan, where you shall find a shelter from the wind you so much dislike.

HASSAN: My little house?

CALIPH: I chose it for you, knowing your disposition.

HASSAN (*with rapture*): Mine, this little house? Mine, this sweet-scented door!

CALIPH: Knock on it and see.

(*Hassan knocks. The door opens and Alder, Willow, Juniper, and Tamarisk appear. Tamarisk, the youngest, has somewhat of a mouse's squeak.*)

ALDER (*to Caliph with prostration*): O, Emir of the Faithful!

WILLOW (*to Caliph with prostration*): O, Redresser of Wrong!

JUNIPER (*to Caliph with prostration*): O, Shadow of God on Earth!

TAMARISK (*to Caliph with prostration*): O, Peacock of the World!

ALDER (*to Hassan with prostration*): Master!

WILLOW (*to Hassan with prostration*): Master!

JUNIPER (*to Hassan with prostration*): Master!

TAMARISK (*to Hassan with prostration*): Master!

(*They stand, their hands in their sleeves, across the doorway.*)

HASSAN: But these are the slaves of the King of the Beggars, who bathed me, and brought back my soul into my eyes.

CALIPH: I have rescued them from the ruin of their master's house as their polite and finished manners deserve.

HASSAN: (*Kneels and kisses Caliph's hand.*)

CALIPH: Say not a word. For the pen of happiness hath written on thy face the ode of gratitude. (*To Slaves.*) Is all ready?

ALDER (*pompously*):   Ready, O Gardener of the Vale of Islam.

WILLOW: Prepared, O Lion. . . .

CALIPH: Enough! Show your master all there is inside his house. Stay with them, Hassan and enjoy. Delicious has been our converse, but Jafar, the Vizier, has been awaiting me some two hours. (*As Hassan is about to prostrate himself.*) No, it is thus Haroun takes leave of his friends.

(*Kisses him on both cheeks. Hassan watches till he is out of sight, pensive. Then he stares out at the fountain. The Slaves bow and open the doors of the Pavilion.*)

ALDER: Fortunate be thy entry!

WILLOW: Prosperous thy sojourn!

JUNIPER: Quiet thy days!

TAMARISK: And riotous thy nights!

The interior of the pavilion is now disclosed. A bed. Fine furniture. A window with a view on the garden.

HASSAN: But to what use shall I put this grand apartment?

ALDER: For the reception of such ladies, Master, as you desire to honour.

HASSAN: Yes, yes. I must visit the market and see. (*Staring at the floor, with a start.*) Wulluhi, what is that?

TAMARISK: The carpet, Master.

HASSAN: One of the wonderful new carpets of Ispahan˙ A hunting scene. The Prince. His followers. Leopards and stags and three tigers, and an elephant—his head only. O, amazing carpet. And everywhere great scarlet flowers, very stiff and fine. O, exquisite carpet. I have never seen so bright a scarlet. Yet it is not so precious as the old carpet hanging on the wall of my shop. Twelve months did I work at the tub boiling sugar to buy that carpet.

ALDER: I pray you, Master. The Caliph said you should particularly observe this mirror with the carven frame.

HASSAN (*looking at himself*): These clothes suit me well. By the Prophet, what a Phœnix I have become! Provided I do not stumble on my sword.

WILLOW: The Caliph said you should not fail to remark this exquisitely upholstered couch.

JUNIPER: The Caliph hoped you would admire these toilet requisites in alabaster.

TAMARISK: The Caliph hopes you will make good use of this very slender whip for our correction.

HASSAN: A whip? For your correction, O slaves of charm? Am I the man to spoil good almond paste with streaks of cochineal?

ALDER: Thou art pleased, O my Master?

HASSAN: Pleased? Look at the acacia tapping at my window; one night it will come in softly and fling its moonlit blossom at my feet. But this is no place for a man to live alone. Without a doubt I must visit the market. They have Circassians; I have always wanted a Circassian. She must be very young. . . . I have not finished the excellencies of the room. These three chests, what do they contain?

ALDER: This chest, O Master, contains your new robes. One of them is embroidered with red carnations and silver bells.

HASSAN: Was there ever generosity like this!

WILLOW: This chest, O Master, contains curtains, hangings, and cushions for the sofa. One of the cushions is embellished with fifteen peacocks.

HASSAN: Fifteen peacocks! And all those peacocks dumb!

JUNIPER: This chest, O Master, contains fresh linen for your bed. All marked with your name.

HASSAN: Marked with my name! And that bed?

TAMARISK: That bed . . .

HASSAN: Doubtless it also contains fresh linen marked with my name.

TAMARISK (*tremulous*): That bed contains a beautiful woman.

HASSAN (*jumping*): What?

TAMARISK: A most beautiful lady. She said she must see you, and gave me ten dinars.

YASMIN (*as Hassan tears aside the curtains of the bed*): Hassan! (*She is dressed in a cloak and veiled. She unveils.*)

HASSAN: Thou!

YASMIN: I came: I hid: I waited.

HASSAN: Why?

YASMIN: Why does a woman hide in the bed of a man?

HASSAN (*furiously*): You dared! Stay here, slaves. Will you leave me at this moment, you fools who let this woman in? (*To Yasmin.*) You dared?

YASMIN: What is there a beautiful woman dare not dare?

HASSAN: But your impudence is vile. Get you back to Selim.

YASMIN: I have left Selim.

HASSAN: Left Selim to come to me?

YASMIN: I found Selim a coward and a fool. I have discovered in you a man of taste and valour. Am I not white enough to follow the caravans of Wealth and Power? (*Flinging out her arms.*) Is this for Selim or that for Selim?

HASSAN: Back to him, and no more words! If he is a fool and a coward, you are nothing but a whore. Get you gone or the slaves shall fling you head foremost down my steps.

YASMIN: I have left Selim because he proved a coward, a fool, a poor man and a nobody. I have come to you because you are rich, famous, and a man of taste. The day you fall into disfavour (may it be far, O my master!) I shall undoubtedly leave you. Till that day you will find me faithful. I am that which you call me—but I bring you a fair merchandise.

HASSAN: I thank you, O seller of yourself. I buy no tainted meat. I beg you seek another market, and that extremely soon.

YASMIN (*rubbing her face and rising lightly*): I did not know I had a taint, O Master. The mirror must deceive me. But merchandise must be well inspected before its inferiority is assured. It must be seen and touched. Will you see and will you touch?

HASSAN (*stepping back*): Oh, away, away! You are as cunning in this act of temptation as in that act of torment. I know you well enough. But I pray you, spare the water from the jug. My fire needs no quenching.

YASMIN (*suppliant*): Be generous. It beseems the Caliph's friend to be generous. If I have made you jealous, do I not offer you a sumptuous revenge?

HASSAN: Rise, take your pardon, and depart. If you need
money, the slaves will give it you at the door.

YASMIN: You are as cold as ice.

HASSAN: You are brazen.

YASMIN: I am brave. Farewell, I see you are not a man
of love.

HASSAN: Farewell. And defile no more the word love
with your painted lips.

YASMIN (*lingering at the door*):   Yet there is little of love's
language that I do not know. When the bird of night
sings on the bough of the tree that rustles outside your
window, and the shadows creep away from the moon
across the floor, I could have sung you a song sweeter
than the nightingales and shown you a whiteness whiter
than the moon.

HASSAN: Ah—go!

YASMIN: Because I was cruel could I not be kind?
Because you can buy my body, can you buy my soul?
Because I am of the people have I no songs to sing?
Because I have sinned have I no secret to impart? Go to
market, O Hassan, and buy your Circassian girl. And
one day you shall say: 'Had Yasmin but lied to me of
love, it were better than this fool's sincerity'.

HASSAN: Ah, leave me!

YASMIN: There are lilies by the thousand in the meadows:
there are roses by the thousand in the gardens, and all
as like as like—but there is only one shape in the world
like mine. There is only one face in the world where
these eyebrows arch and these eyes flash—where the
nostrils are set just so, and the lips are parted thus.
There are rows and rows of young fair girls in the
Caliph's harem and many as fair as I, but none whose

veins are these veins, whose flesh is this flesh, fiery and cool, whose body swings like mine upon the heel. (*Flinging off her skirt.*) Will you see and will you touch? (*Approaching.*) Will you see and will you touch? (*Putting her arm round his neck.*) Will you touch?

HASSAN (*with a shout as he pushes her back*): Slaves, tear off this woman!

YASMIN (*as the Slaves force her back*): Eh, your slaves are violent!

HASSAN (*to Slaves*): Hold her!

YASMIN: But you must let me go.

HASSAN: I will not let you go.

YASMIN: Come, I see you are but a sour fellow, for whom pleasure is but vain. I will take away the hateful. Let me pass.

(*She attempts to escape.*)

HASSAN (*to his Slaves*): Hold her!

(*Alder and Willow grip each an arm. Juniper and Tamarisk grip her ankles. She is held standing. Her cloak falls. She is clothed in short jacket and trousers of white silk with a pattern of blue flowers: her waist is naked, in the Persian style.*)

YASMIN: Ah—what will you do to me? You forgave me.

HASSAN (*to Yasmin*): Ah, I forgave you the insults and all that hour of shame. And Allah shall forgive you your trade if Allah wills. But you have pressed your foul body on mine—you have breathed your poison on my cheek, and twined your snakes (God break them!) round my breast. Prepare then to die, for it is not right for the sake of mankind that you should walk any more upon the roads of earth.

YASMIN (*quietly, but in terror*): To die! What do you mean! No, no! Ah, murder, ah!

HASSAN: Do you hear the fountain dripping—drop by drop—drop by drop? So shall your blood fall on my carpet and colour me more red flowers.

YASMIN (*recovering*): I am not afraid.

HASSAN: Do you expect mercy? I left my mercy with my sweets. For all these years I have been a humble man, of soft and kindly disposition—such a man as the world and a woman hate. But now I shall never again be the fool of my fellows. Now all Bagdad shall know and say: 'We thought Hassan a mild man and a kind man. And behold, he has become powerful and hath cut down the body of Yasmin the infamous who had done him wrong, as a woodman cuts a tree. Yallah, our knees shall bend when Hassan goes driving by!' Yasmin, close your eyes.

YASMIN: Not with the sword, not with the sword!

HASSAN: Let me taste the ecstasy of power. Let me drink of the fulness of life. Let me be one of those who conquer because they do not care.

(*He draws the sword: Yasmin cries out loud.*)

You are Yasmin, the poor, the beautiful, the proud: I am Hassan, rich and passionate and strong. You have hurt me, I will hurt you; it is the rule of the game, and the way of the world. You are the world's own stupendous harlot, and I will cut you clean in two.

(*He swings the sword over his head to strike.*)

YASMIN (*with a shout at once of terror and triumph*): I will not close my eyes! I will look at you. You dare not do it, looking at my eyes!

(*Hassan whirls the sword round.*)

You dare not do it, looking at my eyes!

(*Hassan flings the sword across the room.*)

HASSAN: O, Hassan the Confectioner, thou art nothing but an old man and a fool!

(*Hassan falls upon the bed, his face in his hands. Yasmin comes up to him. The Boys silently disappear. Hassan draws her toward him.*)

(*With infinite tenderness*): Yasmin!

SCENE 2

SCENE: The Great Hall of the Palace. The room is plain, white marble. Ishak alone, in his robes of Court Chamberlain.

Enter Soldiers with the Captain of the Military and the Chief of Police. The Soldiers intone 'The War Song of the Saracens'.

SOLDIERS *sing*:

We are they who come faster than fate: we are they who ride early or late:

We storm at your ivory gate: Pale Kings of the sunset beware!

Not on silk nor in samet we lie, not in curtained solemnity die

Among women who chatter and cry and children who mumble a prayer.

But we sleep by the ropes of the camp, and we rise with a shout and we tramp

With the sun or the moon for a lamp, and the spray of the wind in our hair.

[*Not sung in performance.*]

From the lands where the elephants are to the forts of Merou and Balghar,

Our steel we have brought and our star to shine on the ruins of Rum.

We have marched from the Indus to Spain, and by God we will go there again;

We have stood on the shore of the plain where the Waters of Destiny boom.

A mart of destruction we made at Yalula where men were
afraid,
For death was a difficult trade, and the sword was a broker
of doom;
And the Spear was a Desert Physician, who cured not a few
of ambition,
And drove not a few to perdition with medicine bitter and
strong.

And the shield was a grief to the fool and as bright as a
desolate pool,
And as straight as the rock of Stamboul when their cavalry
thundered along:
For the coward was drowned with the brave when our battle
sheered up like a wave,
And the dead to the desert we gave, and the glory to God in
our song.

CHIEF OF POLICE: That is a splendid song your soldiers
sing, O breaker of infidel bones. Permit an unglorious
policeman to inquire what flaming victory you celebrate
to-day. Such is my loathly ignorance, I knew not the
Caliph's army (may it ever plosh in seas of hostile blood!)
had even left Bagdad.

CAPTAIN OF MILITARY: It is true we have not left Bagdad,
but perchance we have saved it from destruction. For
when the Caliph's Police have allowed a conspiracy to
ripen undetected, it is our duty to mow down the
conspirators. A victory is well worth a song.

CHIEF OF POLICE: Allah, such a song! I thought: 'At
least they have captured Cairo.'

CAPTAIN OF MILITARY: To save Bagdad is better than to
capture Cairo. It is an old song, a glorious great battle

song, and in mocking it thou hast displayed an utter absence of education, thou dragger of dead dogs from obscure gutters.

ISHAK: Is this talk for the High Divan, Captain? Ye have saved Bagdad? Bagdad is no longer worth saving. You rose-petal-bellied parasites of the palace how dare you sing that song?

CAPTAIN OF MILITARY: Allah, these Poets talk in rhyme.

(*Enter the Herald announcing various personages, who enter as he announces them and are motioned to their place by Ishak.*)

HERALD: Abu Said, Prince of Basra, to do homage. Fahraddin, Prince of Damascus, to do homage. Al Mustansir, Prince of Koniah, to do homage. Tahir Dhu'l Yaminayn, Governor of Khorasan, to do homage.

The great caligraphist, 'Afiq of Diarbekir, master of the riqa and the shikasta hands: also of the Peacock style, and of painting in miniature.

ISHAK (*aside*):   Episodes of considerable obscenity.

HERALD: The celebrated Turkoman wrestler, Yurghiz Khan, whose thighs are three cubits in circumference.

ISHAK (*aside*):   As fat as a woman's, but not as nice.

HERALD: Abu Nouwas, the Caliph's Jester. The Rajah of the Upper Ganges, come hither to do homage with a present of 800 bales of indigo.

ISHAK (*aside*):   And never dyed his beard.

HERALD: Hang Wung, the wisest philosopher in China, come hither to study the excellence of the habits of true believers. He is one hundred and ten years old. . . .

ISHAK (*aside*):   And perfectly blind.

HERALD: Anastasius Johannes Georgius, ambassador of

the infidel Empress Irene, mistress till God wills of Constantiniyeh and the lands of Rum, come here on a vain errand. . . .

ISHAK (*aside*): He understands no word, and believes we do honour to his name.

HERALD: Abul Asal, the wandering dervish, come hither to remind kings that they are but dust.

ISHAK (*aside*): Where lies Nushiravan the Just?

DERVISH: The rhyme helps. In the dust.

ISHAK (*aside*): The platitudes of dervishes do not much disturb the beatitudes of kings.

HERALD: Masrur, the Executioner, come hither to make several beggars the dusty equivalents of monarchs. Hassan ben Hassan al Bagdadi, the Caliph's friend.

SOLDIERS: Long live Hassan and the shadow of Hassan and the friend of Hassan ben Hassan al Bagdadi!

ISHAK (*drawing Hassan aside*): Come hither, friend of the Caliph; do not forget that you are the man with the broken lute.

HASSAN: What is a friend?

ISHAK: Has not the Caliph taught you? You have a royal friend.

HASSAN: He is generous: he is gracious: he is intimate. But I tremble before his eyes.

ISHAK: You have found out. No man can ever be his friend.

HASSAN: Alas, that is because he is exalted far above mankind!

ISHAK: Alas, no: but because he uses that supremacy to play the artist with the lives of men.

HASSAN: What do you mean, Ishak?

ISHAK: Have you not seen the designer of carpets, O

Hassan of Bagdad, put here the blue and here the gold, here the orange and here the green? So have I seen the Caliph take the life of some helpless man—who was contented in his little house and garden, enjoying the blue of happy days—and colour his life with the purple of power, and streak it with the crimson of lust: then whelm it all in the gloom-greys of abasement, touched with the glaring reds of pain, and edge the whole with the black border of annihilation.

HASSAN: He has been so generous. Do not say he is a tyrant! Do not say he delights in the agony of men!

ISHAK: Agony is a fine colour, and he delights therein as a painter in vermilion new brought from Kurdistan. But shall so great an artist not love contrast? To clasp a silver belt round the loins of a filthy beggar while a slave darkens the soles of his late vizier, is for him but a jest touched with a sense of the appropriate: and I have seen it enacted in this very room.

HASSAN: But you are his friend.

ISHAK: As you are. It is elegant for a monarch to condescend: it is refreshing for a monarch to talk as man to man. It is artistic for a monarch to enjoy the pleasures of contrast and escape the formalities of Court. . . . But here comes the preceder of the Caliph, the penultimate splendour of the Divan, a man noble without passion, sagacious without inspiration, and weak as a miser's coffee.

HERALD: The Tulip of the Parterre of Government, the Shadow of the Cypress Tree, the Sun's Moon, Jafar the Barmecide.

SOLDIERS: Long live the great Vizier!

HERALD: Let all mouths close but mine. (*Lifting his staff.*)

The Holy, the Just, the High-born, the Omnipotent the Gardener of the Vale of Islam, the Lion of the Imperial Forests, the Rider on the Spotless Horse, the Cypress on the Golden Hill, the Master of Spears, the Redresser of Wrong, the Drinker of Blood, the Peacock of the World, the Shadow of God on Earth, the Commander of the Faithful, Haroun al Raschid ben Mohammed, Ibn Abdullah Ibn Mohammed Ibn Ali ben Abdullah, Ibn 'Abbas, the Caliph!

SOLDIERS:
The Holy, the High-born, the Just One, the Caliph!
The Cypress, the Peacock, the Lion, the Caliph!
From Rum to Bokhara one monarch, the Caliph!

DERVISH (*gloomily*):   A clay thing, a plaything, a shadow, the Caliph!

CALIPH: The Divan is open. Let all mouths close but mine. Our justice to-day will be swift as a blow of the sword. In the Book of the Wisdom of Rulers I read: 'Be sudden to uproot the tree of conspiracy for it scatters far its seed.' Let those whose duty it is fetch him who is called the King of the Beggars from his cell, and let him who did us the great service of capturing alive that dangerous man, step forth into the midst.

CHIEF OF POLICE (*stepping forward*): Lord of the World—but I am dirt.

CAPTAIN OF MILITARY (*simultaneously advancing*):   Lord of the World—but I am dung.

CALIPH: Were you both concerned in his capture? My favour is doubled upon you. Let two robes of honour be brought before my throne.

CHIEF OF POLICE: Sir, I fail to comprehend the presence of this military man. He was but a spectator when I dragged out the King of the Beggars from the gutter of his roof.

CAPTAIN OF MILITARY: O thou civilian, I caught a valiant hold of his legs, despite his heavy and continuous kicks, whilst thou didst but timidly pluck at his sleeve.

CHIEF OF POLICE: Pluck at his sleeve, thou tin-coated murderer! Summon the twenty drops of blood that trickle round thy lank and withered frame and let them mount to thy mendacious cheek!

CAPTAIN OF MILITARY: Thou dropsical elephant!

CALIPH: Enough! I love to hear the speech of heroes, but enough. It is clear the glory is divided. Give me one of those robes of honour, and summon the tailor of the court.

(*The Court Tailor comes running in.*)

COURT TAILOR (*very prostrate*): O Master of the World, O Master!

CALIPH: Slit me this robe in twain.

COURT TAILOR (*moaning as he does so*): Allah is great, Allah is great. Such a well-cut robe: such excellent silk!

CALIPH: Come hither both.

CAPTAIN OF MILITARY (*hanging back*): The glory is all to the Police.

CHIEF OF POLICE: The credit is entirely due to my honourable friend.

CALIPH (*insisting*): Come hither both.

(*They are fitted with half a robe of honour each amid laughter*).

SOLDIERS: Long live those whom the Caliph delights to honour!

CAPTAIN OF MILITARY (*under his teeth*):   Mutinous swine.

CALIPH: And now bring forward the King of the Beggars.

   (*The King of the Beggars is brought in chained hand and foot,
   but still dressed in gold.*)

   The Salaam to my host of yesternight.

RAFI, KING OF BEGGARS: The Salaam, O man of Basra.
   I see thy fellow-merchant in the robes of the Grand
   Vizier. But the negro, that most disgusting negro,
   seems to be absent. To Hassan, my congratulations on
   his advancement.

CALIPH: Thou dost speak with the impudence of a king,
   but thy subjects are taken from thee. They will soon be
   black crows in the pine-wood by the walls.

RAFI: Had I but known thee last night, thou man of
   Basra, whom men call Caliph of the Faithful—had I but
   known thee!

CHIEF OF POLICE: Shall I tear out his tongue?

CALIPH: Let him talk. I have found a man who does not
   flatter me. Let me study the hatred in his eyes.

RAFI: It is not enough for thee to misrule a quarter of
   the world. Thou are not only a foul tyrant, but a mean
   tradesman, thou dog-hearted spy!

JAFAR: It is not decent to let this man continue his
   coarse abuse, O Master. Wilt thou not end him?

CALIPH: He shall end in his time. (*To King of the Beggars*):
   Thy impudence will not redound to thy advantage, Rafi!
   Wherefore dost thou not bite the tongue of insolence
   with the tooth of discretion?

RAFI: I am a man in the presence of death.

CALIPH: There are a thousand paths to the delectable
   tavern of death, and some run straight and some run
   crooked.

RAFI: Cut, scourge, burn, rack thy utmost. Do not I deserve to feel every separate pain of those whom my folly has sent to a cruel death?

CHINESE PHILOSOPHER: I am a hundred and ten years old, and I have never heard a remark in more exquisite taste.

CALIPH: It is well. But before I send thee to a death so cruel that thy conscience shall be fully satisfied in this world and the next, answer me this: Hast thou forgotten that unparalleled lady whom the zeal of my servants ravished from thy embrace?

RAFI: Thou devil of Eblis! Have I forgotten? Have I not prayed thou shouldst forget?

CALIPH: Shall a gallant man forget the name of a beautiful woman? We will look on her, for whom thou didst attempt to raze the central fort of Islam. (*To Attendants*): Bring in this lady, Pervaneh.

RAFI (*in supplication*): O Master of the World! O Master of the World!

CALIPH: Thou changest tone abruptly but late.

RAFI: I was insolent only that her name should be forgotten in thy anger and my death, O Splendour of Islam!

CALIPH: A crafty excuse for impoliteness. Wilt thou now begin to be polite to the tyrant whose coffin was to be nailed over his open eyes? He who hopes for his audience to forget the subject of his discourse should moderate his style.

RAFI: Allah blind me that I may not see her!

CALIPH: Why? Dost thou not love her still? Is not the sight of his beloved to the victim of separation like the vision of a fountain to him who dies of thirst?

HASSAN (*aside*):   But if that fountain be a fountain whose drops are blood?

RAFI: Thou, thou hast held her in thy arms! Oh God, have pity on my soul!

CALIPH: Thou art a most ridiculous man. Thou hast built thy monstrous tower of crime on a foundation of painted smoke. Dost thou imagine I have tasted all the fruit of my garden?

RAFI: Allah has given thee men's bodies, but it is for him alone to torment the soul. By thy faith, O Caliph, speak the truth!

CALIPH: Do I know every slave whom my industrious officials sweep in from the streets? To my knowledge I have never set my eyes on this woman of thine.

HERALD: The maiden Pervaneh!

CALIPH: Let her come before me.
       (*Pervaneh is ushered into the Presence.*)

PERVANEH (*with due reverence*):   O Master of the World!

CALIPH: It is written in the Sacred Law: In the King's presence a woman may unveil, without fear of censure.

PERVANEH: Ah, Master, but only the eagle dare look upon the sun.

CALIPH: Thy speech is proud enough for all the eagles, Lady Pervaneh, and I doubt not thy eyes, which I desire to see, are steady in the blaze of danger. Must I command thee to unveil?

PERVANEH: Alas, Master of the World, my eyes are dim with long confinement in a jewelled cage, and the wings of my soul are numb. Only on the hills of my country where the rolling sun of Heaven has his morning home, only on their windy hills do the women of my country go unveiled.

ISHAK (*to himself, half singing*): The hills, the hills, the morning on the hills!

CALIPH (*to Pervaneh*): I command thee to unveil.

PERVANEH: If thou wilt tear my veil from off my face, I will tear my face before thy eyes.

RAFI: Ah, no! . . .

PERVANEH: Who art thou who dost cry, 'Ah, no!'? Who art thou who dost hide thy face in fettered hands . . .

RAFI: A prisoner.

PERVANEH: Dissembling thy voice . . .

RAFI: A prisoner awaiting death.

PERVANEH: Trembling when I touch thee?

RAFI: A man afraid.

PERVANEH (*in a voice of exaltation*): For thee, Sultan, I raise my veil; and wait thy captive, to share thy destiny.

HASSAN: Oh, Ishak! The fire of the heart of beauty!

RAFI: Leave me, Pervaneh! Walk not upon my path! You do not know what a foul doom is mine.

PERVANEH: Foul dooms? Foul dooms? Rafi, I can forget ten centuries of doom now that I see your eyes again!

RAFI: I conspired against this throne to win you freedom.

PERVANEH: For me you conspired? For me—for me?

RAFI: I would have drowned Bagdad in blood to kiss your lips again.

PERVANEH: O lover!

RAFI (*showing his fettered hands*): Lover indeed!

PERVANEH: There are a thousand eyes round us, O my beloved, but what care I? The voice of the world cries out, 'Thou art a slave in the Palace, and thy lover a prisoner in chains.' (*Embracing him.*) But we have walked with the Friend of Friends in the Garden of the

Stars, and He is compassionate to poor lovers who are pierced by the arrows of this ghostly world. Your lips are the only lips, my lover, your eyes the only eyes—and all the other eyes but phantom lights that glitter in the mist of dreams.

JAFAR: This is sheer heresy.

ISHAK: Then a plague on your religion.

JAFAR: This is Sufic doctrine, and most dangerous to the State.

HASSAN: Then a plague on the state!

CALIPH: Ye who make love in full Divan, can ye yet listen to the voice of the world?

PERVANEH (*dazed*):   They are speaking.

CALIPH: Rafi, King of the Beggars, since after all thou art much entangled in the web of unreality, it is necessary that I ask thee some phantom questions concerning thy apparent acts.

Firstly, dost thou deny thou didst call thyself Caliph of the Unbelievers, and blaspheme thy faith in my presence and in the presence of Jafar, my Vizier, Masrur, the Executioner, and Hassan, my friend?

RAFI: I have nothing to deny.

CALIPH: Dost thou, secondly, deny that thou didst swear in the presence of the same to nail the Caliph of the Faithful alive in his coffin?

RAFI: I have nothing to deny.

CALIPH: Dost thou, thirdly, deny that thou didst scheme this monstrous crime for the sake of a woman?

RAFI: I have nothing to deny.

CALIPH: Rafi, thou art confessed a Blasphemer, a Traitor ... and a Lunatic. It remains to consider thy punishment.

RAFI: As thou wilt.

CALIPH: Thou art brave, but I fear the shafts of unreality will prick thee extremely hard. For thou hast merited not one but a dozen deaths.

RAFI (*with impatience*): What is my condemnation?

CALIPH: For Lunacy to be nailed, for Conspiracy to be stretched, for Blasphemy to be split.

PERVANEH: Ah!

(*Murmurs of horror and satisfaction fill the Court at the announcement of this savage punishment.*)

RAFI: As Allah wills.

PERVANEH (*falling at the Caliph's feet*): Spare, spare, O Master of the World! Mercy! Mercy!

CALIPH: Why dost thou cry 'Mercy' and clasp my feet? Is not pain a fancy and this world a cloud?

PERVANEH (*rising to her feet*): This world is Hell, but those that dig Hell deeper shall find the Hell-beneath-the-Hells which they search for.

CALIPH: Thou hast metaphysic, but hast thou logic? Invent me a reason—one small and subtle reason— why I should show mercy to this man.

PERVANEH: Ah—wilt thou have reasons?

CALIPH: Was not my sentence just?

PERVANEH: Wilt thou have justice?

CALIPH: If I had stood bound before him, would he have listened to my prayer?

PERVANEH: Wilt thou have revenge?

CALIPH: Shall I scorn reason, pervert justice, and put aside revenge—for thy dark eyes?

PERVANEH: Turn thy justice, turn thy revenge on me in the name of the dark eyes of God! They say a woman suffers longer and sharper than a man.

CALIPH: Lady, dost thou mean this with all its meaning,

or say it to implore pity? Beware thy answer! The rack
and whip are ready and near to hand.

PERVANEH (*her arms outstretched*): Then give the word.
Knock off those fetters before my eyes—and nail me
to the wall.

RAFI: Pervaneh!

CALIPH: Ecstasy! Ecstasy! Thou art an ecstatic and
wilt not suffer. I know the thick skins of martyrs. I
refuse.

PERVANEH (*to Rafi*): Alas, what can I do!

RAFI: Let me die! I have seen you again. It is nothing
for a man to die.

PERVANEH: Nothing for a man to die? 'Tis Heaven wide
open for a man to die. But they will tear you, Rafi, Rafi!

RAFI: Shall I fear the pain where you were brave?

CALIPH: What wouldst thou now? I am very patient
with thee.

PERVANEH (*to the Caliph*): I ask so small a boon. I ask
a quick death for my lover.

CALIPH: Thou dost ask a very great boon indeed. For as
thou sayest, what is death? Shall the man who shakes
my kingdom slip into eternity like a thief men catch in
the bazaar? Shall he who does the greater wrong not
suffer the greater pain?

PERVANEH: Just and reasonable, yet there is a holier
thing than reason and justice.

DERVISH (*his orthodoxy disturbed*): A holier thing than
justice?

PERVANEH: Yes, Dervish. There is that which should
not be defiled.

CALIPH: Whither now does thy plea wander?

PERVANEH: O Father of Islam, can thine eyes that love

flowers behold man's body hewn into foul shapes as monstrous as the phantoms that go wailing round the graves? Can thy ears that love the music of Ishak, listen to the gasps of the tormented droning through their bodies like a winter wind among the pines?

CALIPH: Canst thou imagine the lid of a coffin closing on thy open eyes, the sway of the coffin carried to the grave, the crash at the bottom of the pit, the rumble of the earth on the lid, the gasping for breath and light.

PERVANEH: He spoke in fury: but thou dost judge him with a quiet mind. He is a man among men, but thou art the representative of God on earth, the sole Priest of Islam. Thou shalt not order God's image to be defiled.

CALIPH: So you would have me spare him for the sake of the perfection of man's body? O Pervaneh, I am far more likely to spare him for the perfection of woman's.

PERVANEH (*shrinking from the implied menace*): For those that have wits, O Master, perfection is sundered from desire.

CALIPH: You are a woman—perfect—but a woman.

PERVANEH: By the curse of God.

CALIPH: And however much you sunder perfection from desire, from desire your perfection is not sundered.

PERVANEH: I am the slave of thy household to come or go, to fetch or carry, to be struck or slain: but my perfection is not the slave of thy desire.

CALIPH (*softly*): Yet, if you return to my household . . .

PERVANEH (*in fury*): To die.

CALIPH: You would not be forgotten or neglected . . . and your presence would be a consolation and a charm. . . .

PERVANEH: Not to you, frigid tyrant, not to you!

70

CALIPH (*softly*):   Nor yet to the man who let your lover go in peace?

PERVANEH: Is there no shame in the world of Islam? Will you unclothe your lust in full Divan!

CALIPH: You have already given the example. Come, shall I set your lover free?

PERVANEH: I would choke if you touched me, I would choke. Oh, the shame on me, the shame! You sit smiling. It is not me you want but my shame! Is there a God in heaven that lets you sit and smile! But you can set him free. Ah, will you set him free? I am your slave— I am your slave. You can rob me of rope and knife— the very means of death. If you will set him free! I am your slave, what choice have I?

CALIPH: Thou hast not the manners or the heart of a slave. Thou wast brought to my household by violence, a free woman born, and art no slave of mine. In the presence of my Divan I pronounce thee free. Thou art free to come and free to go, free to buy and free to sell, free to wed and free to die—and free to make a choice . . .

PERVANEH: To make a choice? What choice? Between his death and my dishonour?

CALIPH: No, between love and life.

PERVANEH: Explain, O Master of the World!

CALIPH: Between two deaths with torment and two lives with separation. Between a day of love and all the years of life.

PERVANEH: Enlighten my understanding.

CALIPH: I have considered this matter, I have decided this matter. I will speak plain and clear. (*Rising.*) This is my irrevocable judgment from which there is no appeal. I give a choice to Pervaneh and Rafi, the King of the

Beggars, and I grant them till sunset to consult their hearts and make that choice together. If both would live let the lady Pervaneh return forthwith to my harem to be my wife in lawful wedlock, and be treated with all the honour her boldness and her beauty merit. Let the King of the Beggars leave Bagdad, and let these two lovers part for ever till they die.

But if they refuse this separation, I offer them one day of love, from sunset to-night to sunset on the morrow, unfettered and alone, with no more guard than may keep them from self-destruction. But when that day is over they shall die together in merciless torment. In the name of Allah the most merciful, the Divan is closed.

CURTAIN

ACT III

SCENE 1

SCENE: *In the vaults of the palace, outside the cell of the King of the Beggars. Drop Scene.*
Enter Hassan.

HASSAN: Which way? Which way? I am lost in this dark passage. My voice rings round the arches. What's that noise? Is there an army coming? Or are all the prisoners stamping with wrath? . . . No. . . . It is only someone walking. . . . I wonder who! And if this stranger asks me my business what shall I say to him?

ISHAK (*from the darkness*): Who goes there? What dost thou here? What is thy business?

HASSAN: Who calls? I am Hassan, inspecting the security of the imperial prisons. Who art thou?
(Ishak enters.)
Ishak! What are you doing here?

ISHAK: I came here to hear a play more tragic than the mysteries of Hossein to listen to a debate more weighty than the council talk of kings. . . .

HASSAN: You do not mean? . . .

ISHAK: I mean the debate of love and life.

HASSAN: Could you spy on that?

ISHAK: The poet must learn what man's agony can teach him.

HASSAN: Is it then not better not to be a poet?

ISHAK (*bitterly*): Allah did not ask me that question when he made me a poet and a dissector of souls. It is my

73

trade: I do but follow my master, the exalted Designer of human carpets. If he prepared the situation, shall I not observe the characters? Thus I corrupt my soul to create—Allah knoweth what—ten little words like rubies glimmering in a row. As for you, I think you begin to understand the Caliph of the Faithful.

HASSAN: Why speak of him? All men are brutes, you and he and I. I thought that I was kinder than other men— but I was only more afraid. This day is the first day of my exaltation, and see! I have begun it aspiring to cut down a woman.

ISHAK: Are we not both moths of inquisitiveness hovering round the candle of a circumstance? Let us find the cell.

HASSAN: I do not care what I do, for I have lost the meaning of the world. But—who is there?

(*Enter two Guards.*)

ISHAK: The Guard. Leave speech to me. (*To the Guard*): Ho, soldier, whither?

FIRST GUARD (*saluting*): To the cell of the King of the Beggars, my masters, to relieve the Guard.

ISHAK: What, will you stand inside the cell?

FIRST GUARD: Inside, O my masters.

ISHAK: A shame, I say, a shame to spy on a pair of lovers. Will they fly off through the grating or creep through the keyhole?

FIRST GUARD: Ah, you do not know the artfulness of prisoners, my masters. They will bang their heads against the wall, or they will eat their straw. (*To second Guard*): Do they not eat their straw, Mohamed?

SECOND GUARD (*to Ishak*): Oh, sir, they frequently eat their straw.

ISHAK: Chain them, chain them.

FIRST GUARD: We do, my masters, but even then they strangle themselves in their fetters. Do they not Mohamed?

SECOND GUARD (*to Ishak*): I have known them, sir, to strangle themselves in their fetters.

ISHAK: But, as you know, these two have a choice between a life with separation and a death with torment. Now surely they will choose life, and will hardly need a sentry to spear them away from the doorstep of eternity.

FIRST GUARD: I should think so indeed, sir. But you never can tell with prisoners. Prisoners are very obstinate, especially women, are they not, Mohamed?

SECOND GUARD (*to Ishak*): Female prisoners are very obstinate indeed, sir.

ISHAK: But if they do choose their day of love, will they not be free according to the Caliph's promise? Will you still guard them in their cell, O sons of impropriety, lest they eat their straw?

FIRST GUARD (*with a leer*): Nay, we shall stand outside the door, and listen at the grill.

ISHAK: And that is precisely what we intend to do now if you will show us the door.

FIRST GUARD: I don't know whether I could quite do that, sir.

ISHAK (*giving him money*): You are valiant fellows and, I am convinced, considerably underpaid.

FIRST GUARD: Ours is a disagreeable duty, your Excellency, considering the small emoluments.

SECOND GUARD (*holding out his hand for baksheesh*): O, your Excellency, very disagreeable indeed.

FIRST GUARD: This way, gentlemen. (*Moves to the door.*) Hold! Have you the Caliph's pass?

ISHAK: You know I am Ishak and this is the lord Hassan and we go where we will.

FIRST GUARD: Not Jafar himself can enter a cell without a pass.

ISHAK: Mollify thy subordination with this. (*Giving him more gold.*)

FIRST GUARD: It is a bargain on this side and on that.

SECOND GUARD: O, Excellency, since what must be must be, weight the scales of fair play with a little cash.

ISHAK: Not till the close of the transaction. Lead us to the cell.

FIRST GUARD (*leading the way*):   This way, my masters.
                                   Exeunt.

SCENE: *A cell. A grating through which streams the sun-light. A heavy door with a narrow spyhole. Rafi is fettered to the wall, but Pervaneh has not been bound. Two Guards stand immobile on either side of the door. A knock at the door and a shout of 'Guard, oh, guard' is answered by the Guards within. The great bolts are drawn. As the Guards fling the door open Hassan and Ishak are seen. The Guards change places. The door is rebolted.*

RAFI: They have changed our guard for the last time; it will be sunset in an hour.

PERVANEH: Still a long hour before your hands are freed to make me a belt of love. Oh, idle sun, I am weary of thy pattern on the wall. Still a long hour!

RAFI: And still a night and a day before our doom.

PERVANEH: Why is your voice so sorrowful? Your words do not keep step with your decision nor march like standard-bearers of your great resolve.

RAFI: What have I decided? What have I resolved? You came near. I saw the wings of your spirit beating the air around you. You locked the silver fetters around my neck and I forgot these manacles of iron: you perfumed me with your hair till this cell became a meadow: you turned toward me eyes in whose night the seven deep oceans flashed their drowned stars, and all your body asked without speech, 'Wilt thou die for love?'

PERVANEH: Do you repent? Do you unsay the golden words?

RAFI: Put but your lips on mine and seal my words against unsaying!

PERVANEH: I did wrong to make you passionate. I see that in your heart you do repent. I would not have you bound by a moment's madness but with all your reason and with all your soul.

RAFI: Ah, stand apart and veil your face, you who call in the name of reason! You are all a fire for martyrdom: can you hear reason calling from her snows? Oh, you woman, Allah curse you for blinding my eyes with love! Wherefore should I die? The world is full of women as beautiful as you.

PERVANEH: Ah, Rafi.

RAFI: Be silent—be silent! Your voice is the voice of a garden at daybreak, when all the birds are singing at the sun. Forget your whirling dreams, and answer the passionless voice that asks you—wherefore should your lover die?

PERVANEH: I am listening.

RAFI: I am young. Shall I forget to laugh if I continue to live? Shall I spend all my hours regretting you? Shall I not return to my country and comfort the hearts of those that gave me birth? Have I not my white-walled house, my books, my old friends, my garden of flowers and trees? Has the stream forgotten to sing at the end of my garden because Pervaneh comes no more? Shall I not sit beneath the shade and read my book? When I am tired of my book I will lie on my back and watch the clouds. There in the clouds I shall see your face, and remember you with a wistful remembrance as if you had always been a dream and the silver torment of your arms had never been more than the white mists circling round the mountain snows.

PERVANEH (*with growing anger*): And so, wrapped in pleasant fancies, you will forget the woman whose honour you have sold to a tyrant. And so, while I, far from my country and my home, am dying of shame and confinement, you will dream and you will dream!

RAFI: The plague on your dishonour! You are to be the Caliph's wife. Is that worse shame than being flayed by a foul negro? The shame! the selling! the dishonour! A woman's vanity: am I to be tortured to death for this? If I must not have you, do I care whose wife you be? I shall remember you as you are now—rock water undefiled.

PERVANEH: Cold and heartless coward: you are afraid of death!

RAFI: By Allah, I am afraid of death, and the man who fears not death is a dullard and a fool! Are we still making speeches in full Divan to the admiration of the by-standers? Can we not talk one instant with naked souls? If you hate me for fearing death, go your way and leave this coward. Ah, no, no, do not leave me, O Pervaneh! I will die with you. I will die! I will die!

PERVANEH: Shame on you, weak and shivering lover! What is pain for us!

RAFI: You do not see—you do not see! Look at your hands, they shall be torn—ah, I cannot speak of it. I shall see your blood flow like wine from a white fountain drop by drop till you have painted the carpet of execution all red lilies.

PERVANEH: Ah—but will not even your poor love flow deep when I set that crimson seal upon the story of our lives!

RAFI: Alas, you are still dreaming: you are still blind

with exaltation: your speech is metaphor. You do not see, you have never heard the high, thin shriek of the tortured, you have not seen the shape of their bodies when they are cast into the ditch. Come near, Pervaneh. Do you know what they will do to you? Come near: I cannot say it aloud. (*Pervaneh approaches.*) Ah, I dare not tell you. . . . I dare not tell you!

PERVANEH: Tell me, clear and plain.

RAFI: (*whispers in Pervaneh's ear*) . . .

PERVANEH (*covering her face with her hands*):   Ah, God— they will do that! No, no; they will not do that to me!

RAFI: Pitilessly.

PERVANEH (*wildly*):   They will do that!—Ah, the shame of it! They will do that—Ah, the pain of it! I see! I feel! I hear! O save me, Rafi!

RAFI: Alas! Why did I tell you this?

PERVANEH: It is beyond endurance: it is foul. I am between a shame and a shame and there is no escape. . . . But, at least, they shall not do this to you, Rafi. Hush . . . talk low: the soldiers must not hear. (*Glancing at the Guards and whispering low.*) Will you die here between my hands, instantly, and with no pain?

RAFI (*in a hushed voice*):   Quickly! How can you do it? We are guarded—have you a knife?

PERVANEH: My hands will be cunning round your neck, beloved. Did I not say you should die between my hands?

RAFI: Be quick: be quiet: I will cast back my head.

A GUARD (*thrusting Pervaneh back with his drawn sword as she lays her hands on her lover's neck*):   Back, in the Caliph's name!

RAFI (*to Pervaneh*):   Run in upon his sword. . . .

PERVANEH (*shrinking away from the Guard's sword*): I
cannot!

RAFI: Quick—quick! Fall on the sword and save all
shame.

PERVANEH: My breast, my breast: I am afraid . . .
(*Prostrate on the ground.*) I am utterly shamed—I have
missed your death and mine.

RAFI: You have flinched.

PERVANEH: The point was on my breast, and it might
have been all ended for you and me.

RAFI: You have been afraid.

PERVANEH: It would have driven to my heart. Ah, the
woman that I am!

RAFI: It is so small a thing, a pricking of the steel.

PERVANEH: Ah!—it is a little thing, you say? It is like
ice, so sharp and cold. I am a coward.

RAFI: We are both cowards, you and I. The sunlight
changes on the wall from white to gold. It is evening.
Our time has come. Shall we choose life? Shall we
choose the sky and the sea, the mountains, the rivers and
the plains? Shall we choose the flowers and the bees,
and all the birds of heaven? Shall we choose laughter
and tears, sorrow and desire, speech and silence, and the
shout of the man behind the hill?

PERVANEH: Ah, empty, empty without your heart!
(*Weeps.*)

RAFI: Empty as death, Pervaneh, empty as death?

PERVANEH: The wall reddens: the last minute has come:
we must choose.

RAFI: Choose for me: I follow. Did I talk of life? My
heart is breaking for desire of you. If you bid me depart,
I will not live without you. Choose for me—and choose

well. Phantoms of pain! Phantoms of pain! Let me but have you in my arms, and one day of love shall widen into eternity. Who knows? The earth may crack to-night, or the sun stay down for ever in his grave. Who knows—to-morrow—God will begin, and finish the judgment of the world—and when it is all over find you sleeping in my arms?

PERVANEH (*rising slowly to her feet and laying her hands on the shoulders of her lover*): Oh, let us die! Not for my dishonour, Rafi. What is my dishonour to me or you, beloved, or the shame of a girl's virginity to him who made the sea? This clay of mine is fair enough, I think, but God hath cast it in the common mould. O lover, lover, I would walk beneath the walls and sell my body to the gipsy and the Jew ere you should cry 'I am hungry' or 'I am cold'.

RAFI: Die for love of me—for a day and a night of love!

PERVANEH: I die for love of you, Rafi! Behold, the Spirit grows bright around you: you are one with the Eternal Lover, the Friend of all the World. His spirit flashes in thine eyes and hovers round thy lips: thy body is all fire!

RAFI: Comfort me, comfort me! I do not understand thy dreams.

PERVANEH (*her arms stiffening in ecstasy*): The splendour pours from the window—the spirits in red and gold. Death with thee, death for thee, death to attain thee, O lover—and then the garden—then the fountain—then the walking side by side.

RAFI: O my sweet life, O my sweet life—must this mad dreaming end thee?

PERVANEH: Sweet life—we die for thy sweetness. Come, love and die for the fire that beats within us, for the air that blows around us, for the mountains of our country and the wind among their pines; you and I accept torture and confront our end. We are in the service of the World. The voice of the rolling deep is shouting: 'Suffer that my waves may moan.' The company of the stars sing out: 'Be brave that we may shine.' The spirits of children not yet born whisper as they crowd around us: 'Endure that we may conquer.'

RAFI: Pervaneh! Pervaneh!

PERVANEH: Hark! Hark!—down through the spheres— the Trumpeter of Immortality! 'Die, lest I be shamed, lovers. Die, lest I be shamed!'

RAFI: Die then, Pervaneh, for thy great reasons. Me no ecstasy can help through the hours of pain. I die for love alone.

(The cell door opens. The Herald accompanied by Guards enters. Hassan and Ishak are seen.)

HERALD *(entering)*: The Caliph demands your choice.

HASSAN *(falling to his knees)*: O God! O God!

RAFI: Death!

Pervaneh is still in ecstasy when the curtain falls.

SCENE: *Towards sunset of the next day. Another view of the Caliph's garden and of the Pavilion.*

Enter the Caliph with Attendants as Hassan comes from his pavilion.

CALIPH: We were coming to your door to seek you, Hassan, but you have anticipated the knock of doubt by the shock of appearance. Why have you left your house before the nightingale?

HASSAN: Oh, Master of the World, I have sought thee all day, and could not find thee. Thou didst hold the Divan—thou wast hunting—thou wast asleep—thou wast at dinner—and now the hour is near, O Master of the World—but not yet come.

CALIPH: What hour?

HASSAN: The hour of the nightingale: the hour when sun and moon are weighed in the silver scales of heaven: and thy scale of justice moves downward with the sun.

CALIPH: Surely thy head is full of fancies and thy mood perverse. I cannot grasp the shadow of thy meaning.

HASSAN (*throwing himself at the Caliph's feet*): O Master of the World, have mercy on Pervaneh and Rafi!

CALIPH: What—those two? Let them have mercy on themselves. They have chosen death as I am told. The woman has paid me the compliment of preferring torture with her Rafi to a marriage with myself. They have spent a pleasant day together: exquisite food was placed before them, and the surveillance was discreet. They will now pass a less pleasant evening.

HASSAN: Let not the woman be tortured: have mercy on the woman!

CALIPH: Rise, you fantastic suppliant. Do you dare ask mercy for these insolent and dangerous folk whose life was in their own hands—who have themselves pulled down the cord of the rat-trap of destruction?

HASSAN: Had you but heard them—had you but watched as I did while they made that awful choice, you would have forgotten expediency, justice, revenge, and listened only to the appeal of the anguish of their souls!

CALIPH: I doubt it!

HASSAN: They chose so well! They are so young. So terribly in love. I have not slept, I have not eaten, Master! I take no pleasure in my house and garden. I see blood on my walls, blood on my carpet, blood in the fountain, blood in the sky!

CALIPH: Well, well, I will leave you to these agreeable delusions. Abu Nawas has found me a young Kurdish girl who can dance with one leg round her neck, and knows by heart the song of Alexander. I perceive you will be no fit companion for an evening's sport.

HASSAN: It is only for the woman that I implore. Say but one word: the sun will set so soon.

CALIPH (*angrily*): If thou and Ishak, and Jafar and the Governors of all the provinces were prostrate with supplication before me, I would not spare her one caress of Masrur's black hand.

HASSAN (*springing to his feet and making at the Caliph*): Hideous tyrant, torturer from Hell!

CALIPH (*coolly, as Guards seize Hassan*): You surprise me.

85

Since when have confectioners become so tigerish in their deportment?

HASSAN (*terrified*): What have I said! What have I done!

CALIPH: There speaks the old confectioner again.

HASSAN: I am not ashamed to be a confectioner, but I am ashamed to be a coward.

CALIPH: Do not despair, good Hassan. You would not take my warning: you have left the Garden of Art for the Palace of Action: you have troubled your head with the tyranny of princes, and the wind of complication is blowing through your shirt. You will forfeit your house and be banished from the Garden, for you are not fit to be the friend of kings. But for the rest, since you did me great service the other night, go in peace, and all the confectionery of the Palace shall be ordered at your shop. But—a moment. You heard the prisoners make their choice?

HASSAN: I heard.

CALIPH: Inside or outside their cell?

HASSAN: Inside.

CALIPH: Possessing or not possessing my pass?

HASSAN: I knew nothing of the pass.

CALIPH: Then how did you get into their cell?

HASSAN: I do not know, O Master of the World. I slipped in . . . as it might be.

CALIPH: Not the shadow of your shadow could slip into that cell. A slippery palm hath slipped you in, a slippery palm! What motive drew you to that cell?

(*Hassan is silent.*)

CALIPH: An itching curiosity, O son of the Bazaar. A base-born inquisitiveness to hear things which, as you say, concerned you not at all.

HASSAN: I confess.

CALIPH: Do you know the punishment of disobedience?

HASSAN: I fear you are determined on my destruction.

CALIPH: Had I been so determined, Hassan of my eyes, hands that had clutched at the neck of the Caliph of the Faithful would never have clutched again. I make allowance for the purple thread of madness woven in the camelcloth of your character. Indeed, I sympathise with the interest you have shown as to the fate of Pervaneh and Rafi, and as a mark of favour I offer you a place among the spectators of their execution.

HASSAN: Ah, no, no!—that I could never bear to see!

CALIPH: Moreover, as a special token of my esteem, I will not send you to the execution—I will bring the execution here, and have it held in your honour. You dreamt that your walls were sweating blood. I will fulfil the prophecy implied and make the dream come true.

HASSAN: I shall never sleep again!

CALIPH (*to Attendant*):   Take my ring; go to the postern gate, intercept the procession of Protracted Death, and bid Masrur bring his prisoners to this pavilion and slay them on the carpet he shall find within the walls.

HASSAN: Master! Master! Is it not enough? I must go back to my trade and the filth of the Bazaar: I must be a poor man again and the fool of poor men. But preserve, preserve for me, O Master of the World, this palm-grove of memory in the desert of my affliction. Defile not this happy place with blood. Let not the trees that heard thee but yesterday call me Friend bow their heads beneath the wind of anguish! Spare me, spare me from hearing that which will haunt me for ever and for ever—the moaning of that white woman!

CALIPH (*to Guards*): Do not release him till the end. See that he keeps his eyes well opened, and feasts them to the fill. (*Exit Caliph and train.*)

(*The song of the Muezzin is heard, 'La Allah illa Allah,' etc.*)

HASSAN: The sun has set. Guards, oh Guards! (*No answer.*) It is the hour of prayer, do you not pray? I have still a little treasure. (*No answer from the Guards.*) Are you dumb? (*Guards nod.*) But why are you not deaf? (*Guards point to their tongues.*) Ah—your tongues have been torn out! (*Guard points to window of the pavilion.*) What do you point at? . . . Ah, Yasmin!

YASMIN: I have seen and heard behind the lattice. Hassan has fallen from power and favour.

HASSAN (*crazily*): Ah, good, very good, surpassing good! You are at the window—I am in the street. This is a reflection of that. As swans go double in a river, so do events come drifting down our lives.

> Bow down thy head, O burning bright for one night or the
> other night
> Will come the Gardener in white, and gathered flowers are
> dead, Yasmin!

Come now, a sweet lie first, Yasmin: sing a little how you love me. Show me your beauty limb by limb — then bring, ah, bring your new lover—mock my moon-touched verses and call me the fool, the old fool, the weary fool I am!

YASMIN: I will not yet call Hassan a fool. Hassan has fallen from power, but he need not fall from riches. The Palace Confectioner, Hassan, may still become the richest merchant in Bagdad.

HASSAN: Thou harlot, thou harlot, thou harlot!

YASMIN: Why art thou angry? In what have I insulted thee?

HASSAN: Oh, if it were thou about to suffer! If it were thou!

YASMIN (*staring across the garden and forgetting Hassan*):   At last, at last!—the Procession of Protracted Death! I shall see it all!

(*A deep red afterglow illumines the back of the garden. Across the garden towards the door of the pavilion moves in black silhouettes the Procession of Protracted Death, of which the order is this:*

Masrur, naked, with his scimitar.

Four assistant torturers in black holding steel implements.

Two men in armour bearing a lighted brazier slung between them on a pole.

Two men bearing a monstrous wheel.

Four men carrying the rack.

A man with a hammer and a whip.

Pervaneh and Rafi, half naked, pulling a cart that bears their coffins: their legs drag great chains.

Behind each of them walks a soldier with uplifted sword.

Masrur knocks at the door of the Pavilion: the Slaves open and flee in terror at the sight. The light of the brazier glows through the windows. The Soldiers who guard Pervaneh and Rafi unhook the chains that chain them to the cart, and placing their hands on the necks of the prisoners push them in. The four Slaves of the house then appear under the guidance of the man with the whip and lift in the coffins. Lastly, Hassan is taken by his two Guards and forced to enter. The stage grows dark, save for the shining of the light from the windows. In the silence rises the splashing of the fountain and the whirring and whirling of a wheel. The sounds blend

89

and grow unendurably insistent, and with them music begins to play softly. A cry of pain is half smothered by the violins. At last the silver light of the moon floods the garden. Hassan, thrust forth by his Guards, appears at the door of the pavilion. His face is white and haggard: he totters a few steps and finally falls in a faint in the shadow of the fountain. The coffins are brought out, nailed down, and placed in the cart. The Soldiers pull the cart in place of the prisoners, and what remains of the procession departs in reverse order. Masrur only has lingered by the door. Yasmin is clutching at his arm.)

YASMIN: Masrur—thou dark Masrur!

MASRUR: Allah—the woman!

YASMIN: How you smell of blood!

MASRUR: And you of roses.

YASMIN: I laughed to see them writhe—I laughed, I laughed, as I watched behind the curtain. Why did you drink his veins?

MASRUR: A vow.

YASMIN: Will you not drink mine also?

MASRUR: Shall I put my arms around you?

YASMIN: Your arms are walls of black and shining stone. Your breast is the castle of the night.

MASRUR: Little white moth, I will crush you to my heart.

YASMIN *(with a sudden cry of terror, struggling from his embrace a moment after)*:   Ah, let me go. Do you hear them? Do you hear them? . . .

MASRUR: What is there to hear but the noises of the night?

YASMIN *(springing away)*:   The flowers are talking . . . the garden is alive. . . . *(She falls.)*

MASRUR *(stooping to carry her)*:   She loves blood and is

frightened of the moon. She is smooth and white. I
will take her home.

(*Enter Ishak searching for Hassan.*)

ISHAK: Hassan—where doth he lie? Hassan, oh Hassan.
Thou hast broken that gentle heart, Haroun, and I have
broken my lute: I play no more for thee. Ah, why did
they not tell me sooner—I fear his reason may have fled
before I find him. Hassan.

It is he: he lies just as I first saw him: beneath a
fountain, face toward the moon. His life is rhyming like
a song: it harks back to the old refrain. Is life a mirror
wherein events show double?

HASSAN (*half waking from his swoon*): Swans that drift into
the mist. . . .

ISHAK (*bending over him to raise him*): Friend, I am glad
to hear thy voice. Rise, rise, thou art in a pitiable
case.

HASSAN (*faintly*): Let me lie. . . This place is quiet, and
the earth smells cool.

ISHAK: You are alive—you have your reason. Why do
you despair? Be brave: I know you have suffered.

HASSAN: She was brave. Ah, her hands, her hands!

ISHAK: Be silent. Stop dreaming: look into my eyes: listen!

(*Bells are heard without the garden.*)

You hear? The camels are being driven to the Gate of
the Moon. At midnight starts the great summer caravan
for the cities of the Far North East, divine Bokhara and
happy Samarkand. It is a desert path as yellow as the
bright sea-shore: therefore the Pilgrims call it The
Golden Journey.

HASSAN: And what of that to you or me, your Golden
Journey to Samarkand?

ISHAK: I am leaving this city of slaves, this Bagdad of fornication. I have broken my lute and will write no more qasidahs in praise of the generosity of kings. I will try the barren road, and listen for the voice of the emptiness of earth. And you shall walk beside me.

HASSAN: I? (*Rising with Ishak's aid.*) Why save me from a death desired? Why would you force me like a fate to live?

ISHAK: Because I am your friend, and need you.

HASSAN: Oh, Ishak, singer of songs!

ISHAK: Prepare for travel.

HASSAN: I have no possessions.

ISHAK: O pilgrim, O true pilgrim! I have dinars of gold: we will furnish ourselves at the gate. But have you not one thing in your house to take—not one single thing?

HASSAN (*with a great shudder*):   Within that door—nothing. But I have one old carpet that still lies in my shop. Its gentle flowers the negro has not defiled. And yet I dare not seek it.

ISHAK: I will bring it you. You shall stretch it out upon the desert when you say your evening prayer, and it shall be a little meadow in the waste of sand.

HASSAN (*seizing Ishak in a sudden panic*):   Keep close to me: do not leave me! The night is growing wild!

ISHAK: Hold to your reason! It is all stars and moon and crystal peace.

HASSAN: The trees are moving without a wind . . . the flowers are talking . . . the stars are growing bigger. . . .

ISHAK: Be calm, there is nothing.

(*The fountain runs red.*)

HASSAN: The fountain—the fountain!

ISHAK: Oh! alas! it is pouring blood! Come away.

HASSAN: The Garden is alive!

ISHAK: Come away: it is haunted! Come away: come away! Follow the bells!

(*Exeunt in terror.*)

(*The Ghost of the Artist of the Fountain rises from the fountain itself in pale Byzantine robes.*)

FOUNTAIN GHOST: The garden to the ghosts. Come forth, new brother and new sister. Come forth while enough of earth's heavy influence remains upon you—to speak and to be seen. Come forth, and those who are past shall dance with those that are to come.

GHOST OF RAFI (*with the voice of Rafi, the clothes of Rafi, the broken fetters of Rafi, but pale . . . as death*):   We are here, O Shadow of the Fountain.

FOUNTAIN GHOST: Welcome, thou and thy white lady to these . . . haunts. Wander at will. I have scared away the sons of flesh.

GHOST OF RAFI: How were they scared, those two?

FOUNTAIN GHOST: When the water turned from white to red their faces turned from red to white. They ran!

GHOST HIDDEN IN THE TREES: Ha! ha!

GHOST OF PERVANEH: Tell us, O Man of the Fountain, what shall we do?

FOUNTAIN GHOST: Nothing: you are dead.

GHOST OF PERVANEH: Shall we stay in this garden and be lovers still, and fly in the air and flit among the leaves?

FOUNTAIN GHOST: As long as you remember what you suffered, you will stay near the house where your blood was shed.

GHOST OF PERVANEH: We will remember that ten thousand years.

FOUNTAIN GHOST: You have forgotten you are a Spirit.
The memories of the dead are thinner than their dreams.

GHOST OF PERVANEH: But you stay here, by the fountain.

FOUNTAIN GHOST: I created this fountain: what have you
created in the world?

GHOST OF PERVANEH: Nothing but the story of our lives.

FOUNTAIN GHOST: That will not save you. You were
spiritual even in life. But I cared only for the earth. I
loved the veins of the leaves, the shapes of crawling
beasts, the puddle in the road, the feel of wood and stone.
I knew the shapes of things so well that my sculpture
was the best in all the world. Therefore my spirit is still
heavy with memories of earth and I stay in the world I
love. Do I desire to see the back of the moon?

GHOST OF PERVANEH: May not we stay also? May I not
touch the shadow of his lips and hear the whisper of his
love? Shall we be driven from here, O Man of the
Fountain?

FOUNTAIN GHOST: How do I know? Can I foresee?

GHOST OF PERVANEH: Thou, too, dost not foresee. But
what of Paradise, what of Infinity—what of the stars,
and what of us?

FOUNTAIN GHOST: I know no more than you.

GHOST OF PERVANEH: Is the secret secret still, and this
existence darker than the last?

FOUNTAIN GHOST: Didst thou hope for a revelation?
Why should the dead be wiser than the living? The dead
know only this—that it was better to be alive.

GHOST OF PERVANEH: But we shall feel no more pain—
Oh, no more pain, Rafi!

FOUNTAIN GHOST: But you will feel so cold.

GHOST OF PERVANEH: With the fire of love within us?

FOUNTAIN GHOST: You will forget when the wind blows.

GHOST OF PERVANEH: Forget! Rafi, Rafi, shall we forget, Rafi?

GHOST OF RAFI (*in a thin voice like an echo*):   Forget . . . Rafi . . .

FOUNTAIN GHOST: You will forget, when the great wind blows you asunder and you are borne on with ten million others like drops on a wave of air.

GHOST OF PERVANEH: There is a faith in me that tells me I shall not forget my lover though God forget the world. And where shall the wind take us?

FOUNTAIN GHOST: What do I know, or they? I only know it rushes.

GHOST OF PERVANEH: How do you know about the wind?

FOUNTAIN GHOST: Because it blows through the garden and drives the souls together.

GHOST OF PERVANEH: What souls?

FOUNTAIN GHOST: The souls of the unborn children that live in the flowers.

GHOST OF PERVANEH: And how do you know about the passage of ten million souls?

FOUNTAIN GHOST: They pass like a comet across the midnight skies.

GHOST OF PERVANEH: Phantoms shall not make me fear. But what of Justice and Punishment and Reason and Desire? What of the Lover in the Garden of Peace?

FOUNTAIN GHOST: Ask of the wind.

GHOST OF PERVANEH: I shall be answered: I know that in the end I shall find the Lover in the Garden of Peace.

VOICES: And what of Life?

GHOST OF PERVANEH: Who asks, 'What of Life?'

HASSAN

FOUNTAIN GHOST: The spirits of those who will soon be born.

VOICES: We have left our flowers. We know we shall soon be born. What of Life, O dead?

GHOST OF PERVANEH (*with a great cry*):   Why, Life . . . is sweet, my children!

(*The leaves of the trees begin to rustle.*)

FOUNTAIN GHOST: Listen to the trees.

GHOST OF PERVANEH: Is it coming?

FOUNTAIN GHOST: It is the wind. I must go down into the earth.

(*The Fountain Ghost vanishes.*)

GHOST OF PERVANEH: Ah, I am cold—I am cold—beloved!

GHOST OF RAFI (*scarce visible and very faint*):   Cold . . . cold.

GHOST OF PERVANEH: Speak to me, speak to me, Rafi.

GHOST OF RAFI: Rafi—Rafi—who was Rafi?

GHOST OF PERVANEH: Speak to thy love—thy love—thy love.

GHOST OF RAFI: Cold . . . cold . . . cold.

(*The wind sweeps the Ghosts out of the garden, seeming also to ring more wildly the bells of the Caravan.*)

96

SCENE: *At the Gate of the Moon, Bagdad. Blazing moon-light. Merchants, Camel-Drivers and their beasts, Pilgrims, Jews, Women, all manner of people. By the barred gate stands the Watch-man with a great key. Among the pilgrims Hassan and Ishak in the robes of pilgrims.*

THE MERCHANTS (*together*):

> Away, for we are ready to a man!
> > Our camels sniff the evening and are glad.
> Lead on, O Master of the Caravan,
> > Lead on the Merchant-Princes of Bagdad.

THE CHIEF DRAPER:

> Have we not Indian carpets dark as wine,
> > Turbans and sashes, gowns and bows and veils,
> And broideries of intricate design,
> > And printed hangings in enormous bales?

THE CHIEF GROCER:

> We have rose-candy, we have spikenard,
> > Mastic and terebinth and oil and spice,
> And such sweet jams meticulously jarred
> > As God's Own Prophet eats in Paradise.

THE PRINCIPAL JEWS:

> And we have manuscripts in peacock styles
> > By Ali of Damascus: we have swords
> Engraved with storks and apes and crocodiles,
> > And heavy beaten necklaces for lords.

THE MASTER OF THE CARAVAN:

> But you are nothing but a lot of Jews.

THE PRINCIPAL JEW:

> Sir, even dogs have daylight, and we pay.

THE MASTER OF THE CARAVAN:

> But who are ye in rags and rotten shoes,
>> You dirty-bearded, blocking up the way?

ISHAK:

> We are the Pilgrims, master; we shall go
>> Always a little further: it may be
> Beyond that last blue mountain barred with snow
>> Across that angry or that glimmering sea,

> White on a throne or guarded in a cave
>> There lives a prophet who can understand
> Why men were born: but surely we are brave,
>> Who take the Golden Road to Samarkand.

THE CHIEF MERCHANT:

> We gnaw the nail of hurry. Master, away!

ONE OF THE WOMEN:

> O turn your eyes to where your children stand.
> Is not Bagdad the beautiful? O, stay!

THE MERCHANTS (*in chorus*):

> We take the Golden Road to Samarkand.

AN OLD MAN:

> Have you not girls and garlands in your homes
>> Eunuchs and Syrian boys at your command?
> Seek not excess: God hateth him who roams!

THE MERCHANTS (*in chorus*):

> We take the Golden Road to Samarkand.

HASSAN:

> Sweet to ride forth at evening from the wells,
>> When shadows pass gigantic on the sand,
> And softly through the silence beat the bells
>> Along the Golden Road to Samarkand.

ISHAK:

> We travel not for trafficking alone;
>> By hotter winds our fiery hearts are fanned:
> For lust of knowing what should not be known,
>> We take the Golden Road to Samarkand.

THE MASTER OF THE CARAVAN:

> Open the gate, O watchman of the night!

THE WATCHMAN:

>> Ho, travellers, I open. For what land
> Leave you the dim-moon city of delight?

THE MERCHANTS (*with a shout*):

>> We take the Golden Road to Samarkand!
>> (*The Caravan passes through the gate.*)

THE WATCHMAN (*consoling the women*):

> What would ye, ladies? It was ever thus.
> Men are unwise and curiously planned.

A WOMAN:

> They have their dreams, and do not think of us.
>> (*The Watchman closes the gate.*)

VOICES OF THE CARAVAN (*in the distance singing*):

> We take the Golden Road to Samarkand.

CURTAIN

THE END